You Are Loved, Too

Also by Ron Johnson

You Are Loved

You Are Loved, Too

by

Ron Johnson

NATIONAL WRITERS PRESS

To contact the author please e-mail at
rjohnson@churchhookey.com or
visit www.churchhookey.com

Published in the United States of America by
National Writers Press
17011 Lincoln Avenue, #421
Parker, Colorado 80134 USA

Printed in the United States of America by
KIMCO PrintingDenver, Colorado USA
Special Thanks to Craig McKillip; KIMCO Representative

Cover Design by
NZ Graphics
1445 South Quail Court
Lakewood, Colorado 80232

LIBRARY OF CONGRESS CATALOGING-IN-PUBLICATION DATA

Johnson, Ron
You Are Loved, Too by Ron Johnson
International Standard Book Number: 0-88100-132-5

1. Inspirational   2. Religion/Bibles   3.Self-Acctualization/Self-help
I. Title   95069511

TABLE OF CONTENTS

Dedication

This book is dedicated to you as well as to my parents: Mr. and Mrs. Grady L. Johnson and to my wife's late parents: Mr. and Mrs. L. R. Schahn. We all need those valuable influences in our lives in order to live an effective and fulfilled life. And no life is complete without knowing who you are, where you came from, why you are here and the greatest reality of all, *You Are Loved, Too* by the great God who made you.

> *Greater love hath no man than this, that a man lay down his life for his friends"* (St. John 15: 13 KJV).

I am deeply indebted and thankful for these parents who have shaped my life and helped me and many others to realize just how much God really does love you and me. You Are Loved, Too.

Foreword

by Nancy Jean Schahn Johnson

At the age of 5 years old, I walked down the aisle of our home church and told my pastor I wanted Jesus to live in my heart. Did I understand everything about the Bible and God? No, of course not. However, I had heard my dear parents pray earnestly to God, and at this early age, I knew he answered prayer. I knew already I was safe in the arms of a loving God.

Over the years, I have come to the realization that people of the world are in very different stages of life in relationship to God. Some people have heard of God but have no desire to accept him. They may have even embraced other beliefs by those who claim to be God. Then there are those who know God is real but may or may not have accepted him into their lives. Last, there are those who know He is real and have experienced Him daily and intimately.

After reading Ronnie's writing for almost 38 years I can say there has always been one theme and one purpose. It is to tell everyone that God loves you and is always there for you, whoever you are, and wherever you may be. So I can say without doubt, this book, You Are Loved, Too, is for everyone.

(Nancy, Ronnie's wife, has been an elementary school teacher for over 30 years and was elected *Teacher of the Year* by her local school in Aurora, Colorado a few years ago. She and Ronnie actually grew up together in the same church nursery at their home church in Orange, Texas, the Cove Baptist Church. It was there that Ronnie and Nancy were baptized. It was also where Ronnie was licensed into the gospel ministry, ordained as a minister and where they were married by their long time pastor, mentor and friend, Rev. W. W. Kennedy).

*CHRISTIAN
LIVING*

"...life is found in its quality and not its quantity..."

ALIVE, BUT NOT REALLY LIVING

Her eyes gave that forlorn look. She was relating how she had lost her husband of fifty years in marriage. Now and then she would look down as she spoke. There was a distinct grimace upon her face. One could readily tell she had been through a whole lot over his dying years.

"You know," she made herself talk, "he was a really good husband and was faithful all our fifty years we were together. His death was still very untimely, as always. I've had to make some pretty big adjustments since he's been gone, 'cause he did everything, it seemed."

For a moment only time and space filled our conversation looking each other in the eyes with unspoken words, you might say. She knew I cared as I listened intently, and I knew she was still hurting badly, even three years since his passing.

"Ron, I did discover something through the loss of my husband, though."

"What's that?" I asked.

Jill quickly replied, "Someone can be alive and not be living."

"How do you mean?" I questioned her more.

"Well, Jerry was so sick for so long that it dawned upon me that he was just there. He had no quality of life, or hope for a tomorrow. He was just there for so long. Nothing meant anything to him. Like I say, he was alive, but not really living. It was heartbreaking."

The day I heard this little lady say these words, I thought about how many people in this world are alive, but are not really living. Many of them are in this condition and they are perfectly healthy, maybe even wealthy. But they are alive, not really living.

So many people's marriages are the same way. They are alive, but not living. People's work, alive, but not living. How sad to think that people go for years in life so alive, and yet so dead at the same time.

In Christianity and especially the church, there can be life, but not really living. People are breathing, going, doing, performing, singing, preaching, even ministering, teaching, but they are not living. There's a staleness. An emptiness. There is mere existence without any excitement, energy or true living going on.

What a tragedy! To be alive. but not living. Certainly, if someone is ill or incapacitated, they cannot help this. If you're dying, you can't be living, in most cases. But when you're alive, living and still not really living because you've lost your purpose and reason for being here, that's sad.

Remember the Lord said, "I've come that you might have life and have it more abundantly." That word abundant means "wave after wave." Is there anything more powerful than the ocean's waves of water which come roaring upon the shores during a terrible storm? Man, what power! What life! What energy! The ocean is alive and really living then.

"If you're green," someone said, "you grow; but if you're ripe, you'll rot."

Are you alive? Or, are you living? How is your faith? Better still, how is your living? How's your energy?

Nothing I can think of that can be any worse is for you and me to be alive, but not really be living. Everyday that God gives us is special. Those twenty four hours are such a gift. Meeting people, seeing our kids off to school, meeting business challenges, even paying those bills on the 30th of every month, facing problems and attempting to reconcile relationships—all of these are gifts. We can thank God we have things to worry about. No worrying, no living!

When you cease to care about anything, there is no reason to live. If you are really praying hard for someone in your world, you can be sure you are very much alive and living. If you're going through an awful struggle either with your own life, your family's problems, or with a friend's heartache, you're living, you're not just alive.

Oliver Wendell Holmes once said, "Most of us go to our graves with our music still in us." How tragic that millions of people live every day who are alive, but keep their music locked up inside them. They are alive, but they're not living. They have lost the zest and vigor for life, their work, and their purpose for even being here. When this occurs people really are just alive, but not living.

It was through the loss of His blood, His own life, that Christ the Messiah brought hope and peace and forgiveness of sin. How strange! In death and in the horror of hell itself, the Lord brought forth real living for you and me. Even in death he lived. No wonder "in Him we live and move and have our being." As a Christian we have every reason in this world to be both alive and living.

Remember Samson? He lost his unusual strength when he was betrayed by Delilah and his head was shaven. He was alive, but he was no longer living. The Philistines even put out his eyes. After being placed in a prison house in Gaza to grind, his hair began to grow again.

When his hair was long God endowed him with this unusual strength. In the end he took his own life by destroying many Philistines. God granted him the strength to pull a building down on the Philistines. The tragedy here is that such a mighty man of strength and power reached a point in his life where he was alive, but he was not living.
I am convinced that I am talking to a lot of people who read this

article like you and I. We find ourselves alive, but not really living. We all reach that point at times in our lives. It's like a wall. We are not as inspired or motivated to do what we've done before. This can happen to all of us. The music is there but neither we nor anyone else is sharing its rhythm or enjoyment.

You can be alive and living. You and I have inner God-given power to do more than we could ever imagine ourselves. "<u>With</u> God all things are possible." Remember it's <u>with.</u> Our source of power and energy and living, real living, comes from the Lord.

I hope you've read the book, *Tuesdays With Morrie*. It's a very simple yet deep little book about a professor and his dying days. The author is one of his students who visits Morrie on Tuesdays. The student who sat under this professor some years earlier records the wit and philosophy about living and dying from his old professor. This true account reveals just how mature some people can be upon their death bed.

Morrie is dying, but he is very much alive and living. He teaches us that life is indeed precious, and everything we do has meaning and purpose here. He also teaches exactly what this little lady taught me when she said, "You can be alive and not really be living."

Morrie reminds us that life is found in its quality and not in its quantity; some people live to an old age, and yet they never lived, they were only alive. How sad! It is death itself to live for years and years and never really be living. No goals, no aspirations, no personal achievements or accomplishments, people just living and then dying.

The Apostle Paul sums it up for us when he declared: "I am crucified with Christ: nevertheless I live; yet not I, but Christ lives in me: and the life which I now live in the flesh I live by the faith of the Son of God, who loved me, and gave himself for me." Let Christ not only be alive in you, but let Him live through you. Then the living is much more easy and fulfilling. I'll choose living above just being alive any day. May God help each of us to live for Him and His glory until our own dying day.

"...I could have just given a little more effort and it would have made all the difference in the world - for me, and for others."

IF I COULD JUST GO BACK AGAIN

My long-time friend, the prophet, lives alone in the woods of Southeast Texas. He is a very quiet, wise Christian man who I have come to greatly admire over the years.

We attended college together in the late sixties. His name is Joe. He has taught me so much over the years about the simple things of life and especially about people and their human nature. Joe is not very impressed with what's in, such as style or name brand stuff. To him what is "in" has more to do with honesty and character and just plain good-heartedness.

It's been a number of years now that he said it, but it has never left my mind and my soul. We were eating lunch together and he just made a passing comment, "Ronnie, if I could just go back again...if I could just do it all over on that basketball court, I really think I would do it differently."

"Joe," I asked intently, "what do you mean exactly?"

"Well, Ronnie, you can't call back the past, you can only carry the past with you into the future. And I know," he continued so pensively, "that if I could just go back again I would have definitely changed things: I would have stayed a little longer at practice on my own; I would have practiced more free throws than I did; I would have worked harder on my jump shots, and God only knows how many more things I know I would have taken much more seriously."

"Well, you don't blame yourself for your team not winning state do you? After all, you did come in second."

"Oh, no! I'm really not even thinking about that. I'm really think-ing about a lot of things that I now look back on and I could have just given a little more effort and it would have made all the differ-ence in this world—for me and for others. No! No! I'm not think-ing just about basketball."

Joe is truly the deepest thinking human I have ever been around. Most people accept just about everything they hear on the news and otherwise; Joe thinks in a different sphere altogether. He is not an antagonist; he just thinks more than most of us.

Once he told me, "Ronnie, have you ever noticed that a real poi-sonous snake you meet on a path will usually avoid you if you give him time to scoot away? He's smart. He doesn't want any more trouble than you do."

Wow! What a thought! And he's right, too. I wonder how many people have been bittten by a poisonous snake who could have avoided them in the first place?

If I could just go back again...what a profound statement. Ever since Joe made that statement some twenty years ago, I think about it often. It made me think about myself. How many times could I have been a better student of God's Word? How many times could I have gone out of my way just a little more to help a friend or a stranger, or even a family member? How many times could I have dropped to my knees and said a simple prayer to God in heaven? How many times could I, too, have practiced harder at what I was working at, or even playing at? But now it's too late—at least too late to change the past.

Paul, in one of his little notes to a church, wrote, "Brothers, I count not myself to have apprehended: but this one thing I do, forgetting those things which are behind, and reaching forth unto those things which are before, I press toward the mark for the prize of the high calling of God in Christ Jesus."

That's it! That's the answer. We can't go back. So you and I must go forward now and try to have as few regrets as we can about our devotion to our work and family and to others who need us. Our past is over. Yesterday is smoke; tomorrow we have new fires to burn, new horizons to scale and new challenges to meet and conquer.

Let's practice now and stay the extra time it takes to achieve what we can for God's glory and for the sake of humanity.

The great pastor for years in San Antonio, Texas, Dr. Buckner Fannin, used to employ this quote frequently:

How I wish there was some wonderful place,
Called the Land of Beginning Again;
Where all our heartaches, and all our mistakes, and all our poor selfish griefs,
Could be dropped like a shabby old coat at the door,
And never be put on again.

If I could only go back again, that thought lives within me year after year. But never forget, we serve Someone so wonderful Who never had to say that. No, He said, "It is finished." Thank God He didn't have to go back to complete anything.

I hope you will be reinspired to stay longer and work a little harder and do just a little more than you ever have before for others and for the glory of our great God and King.

You and I have today, not tomorrow, not yesterday—<u>today</u>! Let's make the most of it.

"All men knew what he stood for and who he stood for."

THE CONSENSUS

As we study the scriptures we all find that the Holy Spirit just knocks us over sometimes with a mini message from a familiar passage which we've read a hundred or more times before. Why? Because the scriptures would become very dull and lifeless if the Bible was just any other text book or novel inspired by man only.

I often read the 11th chapter of the Gospel of Mark. This time, however, one of those mini messages leaped out into my heart. This particular chapter is one of my favorites in scripture.

After the Lord curses a fig tree and cleans out the temple from the money changers in this chapter, his critics want to know why and where his authority comes from to do the things he does.

Jesus simply tells his critics, "I'll tell you if you can first tell me if John's baptism was from heaven or from men." The critics realized as they reasoned together that if they say it's from heaven, then he will ask them why didn't you believe. If they say it's from men, the critics then would fear the people: **for all men counted John, that he was a prophet indeed**.

And there it is, at least for me. There is the mini message, **the consensus**. What a wonderful consensus, too! Here is a man who has so lived his life and demonstrated such character that "**all** men counted John a prophet indeed."

You've heard the expression a player is a consensus All-American for football or basketball; it simply means that most agree the player is just that good. Consensus comes from the Latin words, **con**, meaning with and **sentire**, meaning to feel or think. With both feeling and thinking everyone agreed long ago that John was a prophet, indeed.

I can't help but ask, what is the consensus of people who know me? Who know you? John had so lived his life representing God that his life became a message that was living in the hearts of all men. No doubts about his faith, his passion and his resolve. All men knew what he stood for and who he stood for. His disposition mirrored the Lord. He was revered as a prophet.

Do you know of many TV preachers who are revered as John was? How many pastors or missionaries or teachers or Christians today command that kind of a consensus? Do people take note of us like they did the early disciples that we have been with Jesus? And imagine, if we think most of these TV preachers are too syrupy selling their pills, diet plans and prosperity thinking today, what does God think?

I love those words of John who writes, "By this shall all men know that you are my disciples, if you have love one to another." There's no second-guessing, no question whatsoever about being a godly person on this earth when people see us with a genuine love for other people. It is clear-cut where we stand, and who we stand for by our compassion and sincere care for others.

Love is a test tube, really; what shakes out in the end reveals who we are. Love reveals this consensus. She's for real. He's for real. That person stands for God and righteousness. Or, something just doesn't add up. There's a rat in the woodpile somewhere.

No wonder Immanuel Kant declared, "Two things fill my mind with ever-increasing wonder and awe...the starry heavens above me and the moral law within me."

That moral law comes out, too. Even a small child comes to a consensus about adults. We can't fool them. They see our colors. They know our ways. We notch out our own consensus when all is said and done.

Probably no story in the Bible reveals more about **the consensus** of a person's life than that of Samuel when Saul is in search of his father's donkeys. He travels quite a way with a servant in search of the animals. When Saul finally chooses to give up and return to his father's house, his servant remembers a seer (prophet) whom he thinks can help. The servant explains:

> Look, in this town there is a man of God; he is highly respected, and everything he says comes true. Let's go there now. Perhaps he will tell us what way to take.

> — 1 Samuel 9:6 (NIV)

Wow! What an influence Samuel had back then. This servant and Saul were nowhere close to home, yet the servant had heard about this extraordinary man of God with such wisdom and spiritual insight; word had traveled. Word gets 'round when God is in someone's life for real. And God had his hand upon Samuel.

Later Saul and his servant asked some young ladies who were going to draw water about this seer, where they might find him, and they knew exactly who they were asking about. They may have never darkened the door of Samuel's church, but they knew the character of the man who led the church. They said:

> He is. He is ahead of you. Hurry now; he has just come to our town today, for the people have a sacrifice at the high place...

> — 1 Samuel 9:12 (NIV)

I think that it was obvious that all men back then counted Samuel as a prophet indeed, just like John the Baptist. The consensus was clear. Confident. Concluded. No more interrogation needed; enough evidence required convicting them both that they were men of God. That's spine tingling to me. Those Middle Eastern, tawny girls going to that well or river for their water on a mundane chore knew exactly who they were asking about. They knew Samuel was a man of God. He was not just another preacher in town. He had made his mark on both the commoners and the city leaders of that day.

What an influence! What a man of God! The word really had spread. No one had to question who this man was.

What an aura must have encircled this giant of a man of God in the ancient world! When I was growing up as a young minister, there was an aura about an evangelist called Manley Beasley. I heard him preach on several occasions, once at an evangelistic conference in Fort Worth, Texas.

I shall never forget one rainy night after he had brought an incredibly moving, stirring message to all of us preachers; we came to a stop light near the Tarrant County Convention Center. I was riding with other ministers in a car. I was looking out my window with raindrops and mist almost concealing my view, and there he was, standing and waiting to cross the street. Manley that night was all alone in the cold dampness of the night, totally away from all the thousands that were in the great convention center. But the aura, the nimbus was still there. You could just feel it. You knew the consensus. And he never said a word; he was just standing on a street corner waiting for a light to change.

"How we get our priorities so mixed up down here."

NOTHING ELSE MATTERS

Only once in awhile my lovely wife of almost four decades, now and then will burst forth with a statement that cries louder than a huge clap of thunder in your ear. It was only recently, too, that she came out with one of those classic comments that only Nancy can author.

I was tired and kind of annoyed by a terrific schedule of things I thought I just had to get done on the weekend. Then, I was at the same time dealing with two grandchildren and a whole bunch of other issues that just crept up on me. Besides all this I was having trouble with my computer and getting through on an online test I wanted desperately to finish. Just wasn't meant to be!

Dal (Davin) as we now call him, our six-year-old grandson, kind of knocked over a tray filled with dishes right off the kitchen counter. That's right! Everything broke: plate, cup, bowl, you name it, he massacred the whole kitchen. Glass was everywhere. Food and drink went everywhere. I couldn't even think of trying to conjure up a bigger mess. Yes, I wanted to curse, but I didn't. Don't judge me; you would have wanted to as well!

Dal is one of those hands-on children who gets into everything and then even more. You don't think so? Just keep him. When he comes over we put our seat belts on, hold our breath, make sure our homeowner's insurance is current, clothe ourselves with any armor we can find, and love every single minute he's with us, he and his little brothers, Blaine and Hayden. They are three of the loveliest little kids God ever made. There are no words to describe our love for these three boys.

This particular weekend I seemed to have had so much on my mind. Ever have those kinds of days or weekends? I had a list of things that I'd put off forever, so I had made up my mind that I was going to get them done. Over! History! But it just wasn't going to happen. Dal and Blaine kept me so busy I didn't know what to do. They were like hurricane Ivan. They blew in and I blew over. Wow! What a crazy, crazy weekend!

After they left and things settled down, I bemoaned to my wife how little I had accomplished over the weekend and how discouraging it was to have so many tasks I wanted to finish and didn't finish a one. And Nancy said, almost as though it was a voice from heaven itself, "Ronnie, when it comes to those children, nothing else matters. I know you wanted to get a lot of things done, but nothing else matters really, does it?"

"No," I agreed, "Absolutely nothing. They are the most important things in this world to us; them and our children and family."

You know, I could not get that off my mind for the longest time. "Nothing else matters." Boy! How we get our priorities so mixed up down here. These little guys and others will run this world one day. Everything we do now to teach them, to embrace them, and to guide and love them is so paramount.

In that great movie, *The Scent of a Woman*, I just love how the lieutenant defends the young man at Baird College. The young man would not give up his friends by squealing on them, so the lieutenant comes to his rescue in front of the whole faculty and student body. He makes a memorable statement there that should never be forgotten. He declares to the presiding headmaster, "The last thing you want to do to this boy or any other boy here is to amputate his spirit, because there is no prosthetic for that."

Children are just going to turn over milk, spill juice on the new carpet, mark on furniture, scratch tables, stain their clothes, but all that can be replaced. But their spirit can't be. This is the last thing that should ever be amputated, 'cause there just isn't any prosthetic for our spirit. Right? How true! How very, very true!

"Nothing else matters." Wow! What a statement! This is why that Man lived some two thousand years ago, walked up that hill and gave His life; because He wanted to make spirits right, to heal human hearts. Nothing else matters but you and me. That's why he gave his very all. Why? Because we mean everything to Him, you and me.

You can be sure that Nancy's words will always hold true when it comes to a human life and human soul—nothing else, absolutely nothing else matters more. No work, no business matter, no task, no job or pressing appointment—NOTHING!

"...life should be lived with sensible and purposeful and meaningful outlines each day..."

RONNIE, YOU NEED AN OUTLINE

I write a new manuscript, I guess like all authors every so often, and place it away for awhile and let it kind of simmer. Some time ago, I wrote a nifty little book and had a local editor go through the manuscript and "rip it apart" at my request. Most of us writers don't really like the criticism, but we know it is a necessity if we are going to be the most efficient in our communication with our readers.

After my first consultation with her, in the nicest way she could, she blurted, "Ronnie, you need an outline!"

My instant reply was, "You're exactly right. I just picked up my pen and began writing. And I just couldn't put the pen down until I was finished; however, I know you're right. I just needed to hear it from someone like yourself."

Deep down inside me I knew why I wrote this way. I have, along with ADD (Attention Deficit Disorder), what is called Hyper Focus. When I go into these moods, or zones as I call them, I become so focused that nothing else around me seems to matter. Then after I finish what I'm doing (which happens when I write in most cases) I can't believe what I've done—seriously. No, I'm not crazy. In fact, Bill Gates and Charles Schwab and many other famous and not so famous people have this same syndrome.

You know, I got to thinking about that word "outline." Webster's says, "To outline is to indicate the chief features or parts of." So I went back to the basics. Even the Lord when He was on this earth talked about the cost of building a house and going to war. He said one must first count the cost before a house can be built. Otherwise, if a person only gets halfway through, people will laugh at such poor planning. The same is true with a war, why go up against an enemy unless proper strategy is first designed and planned. We must always consider the strength of the enemy and our own.

Writing demands fundamentals. You know: Theme, Introduction, Main Body, and Conclusion.

I also got to thinking about the outlines in our world which affect us every moment and every day and every year of our lives. The design by our Creator of this universe is a masterpiece of an outline. The homes we live in were drafted by someone who made a blueprint of the floor plan which we walk through every day. The cars we drive are first conceived by those engineers at Honda and General Motors and Ford and others. The jewelry on our bodies, the clothes we wear, the dishes we eat from, and the computers we e-mail on all began with some kind of an outline or architectural drawing.

Every skyscraper begins with that rendering, that diagram, long before it becomes a reality. My dad for years now has drawn upon a piece of paper a simple plot or outline of what he envisions will be built by my brothers. And he has built many buildings from a simple outline, which have become successful commercial stores and shops and places for business in Southeast Texas.

As a former pastor, I now look back and remember that my sermons were far better messages when I took the time to first allow God to impress upon me an outline long before I built the actual text on which to speak.

"Ronnie, you need an outline." You know, those words really pierced my heart. Why? Because life should be lived with sensible and purposeful and meaningful outlines each day of our lives. From our work to our diets, from our workouts to our play, from our entertainment to our continuing education, we should take seriously an outline to make our own world more efficient and fulfilling.

How does your day begin? How much time alone do you allow

yourself each day? Look back over just one week which you have lived and scan your calendar and see just how much time you set aside for you.

Just think with me a moment longer. When you consider the outline of just one single cell of the body, it is mind-boggling how God mapped out our skeleton. In the adult body there are 200 distinct bones. We have long bones, short bones, flat bones, mixed bones and surface bones. One only needs to read Henry Gray's book on anatomy to think twice about a Greater Power. What an outline! What a motif God has defined in the giving of life in these skeletons! It is truly overwhelming.

No wonder the Psalmist declared, "I will praise You; for I am fearfully and wonderfully made..." (Psalm 139:14).

You know, I do need an outline. I need a beginning and an ending. I need a track to run on. How about you? It is the outline, that plan that makes our world easier, more proficient, more exciting believe it or not. Let's start our day with God and prayer, and let's close it with God and prayer. Do you need an outline? I do.

"It is amazing to me how maturity and righteousness go hand in hand..."

RIGHTEOUSNESS

We really don't hear much about righteousness anymore. But I think we should. In scripture we are taught, "Righteousness exalts a nation, but sin is a disgrace to any people."

As we work with families and individuals week after week helping them in their legacy planning and intergenerational planning, it becomes so obvious just how righteousness plays a part in what we try to accomplish with them.

Many people do not have the one thing we are looking for when it comes to such planning. It is a word that is second nature for us who are in estate legacy planning. It is the word, maturity. Maturity means fully grown or developed. It comes from that Latin word, *Maturus*, with the "a" long and the first "u" long as well. So it is pronounced like, May-two-rus. And it means of all things, ripe.

It is amazing to me how maturity and righteousness go hand-in-hand when people are planning for their heirs and their beneficiaries. This is so obvious. People who are ripe enough, mature enough to sit down and take time to plan for their children and grandchildren and great grandchildren always have a deep desire to do what is "right" for those they love the most.

I like what Twain said, "Do what is right, it will gratify most people and astonish the rest."

I think even some family members will be astonished when they realize how Mom and Dad or Grandma and Grandpa "got their house in order" before their passing; also how they provided so efficiently for their family's financial future. Why? Because most people leave things in a mess after they are gone. More than 70% of Americans die without a will.

Now and then people will come to my associate, and me, and we realize almost immediately just how far off center they are. It is impossible to help them plan their estate or anything else, for that matter. The Big Five, as we call them, has a definite missing link. The Big Five are a "must" for estate legacy planning:

   <u>Knowledge</u>: people must have learned enough to start asking the right questions. People have the answers already in most cases; they just do not know the right questions to ask to set up the estate plan.

   <u>Maturity</u>: They must have become "ripe," they must have truly reached a place in their lives that they have faced their mortality. They are fully grown in their thinking to accept a 9/11 no matter what the consequences may be. And they want their house in order for the unexpected. It really does take a mature person to look life right square in the eyes and face it with serious planning in the event death occurs or incapacity comes about.

   <u>Money</u>: Naturally, an individual or family must have enough assets to do estate legacy planning. Assets pass by law or by contract, or by will. In our state, Colorado, people with property in excess of $50,000 must go through probate provided they do not have the right legal documents in place. Estate planning really is more than about money; it has much to do with emotions and relationships and sentiment. However, we have found over the years that "gold is always thicker than blood," and money does matter in estate planning strategies.

   <u>Time</u>: There are so many people whom we visit who complain about how much time they have had to take to set up their estate plan. However, it really is one of the most important things a person will ever do on this planet. Time is essential for a proper plan to be implemented. One of my family's favorite sayings is the one by Robert Greene, "Time and tide wait for no man." Many people do procrastinate until it is too late to set up an estate plan. They really don't do anything right or wrong; they just do not take the time to do anything.

<u>Love</u>: In estate legacy planning, this is the glue which holds everything together. It is also the very thing that drives people to do what is "right" for those they are transferring their assets to. When we hear people say, "I want my family to be taken care of," this is a key that unlocks many doors for us to guide families toward the needed planning for their future generations.

I looked up the root term in Hebrew for righteousness. It is a word which actually means "clear self." What a picture of people who really do "get their house in order" when it comes to estate planning. People must be very open with themselves and with others if this is ever going to be accomplished. It's like "coming clean."

Estate Legacy Planning actually demands a "clear self." It demands being honest with your spouse, with your family, with a team of professionals, with God, and most importantly, with yourself.

People often ask me, "Ronnie, what do you mean by legacy?" I explain that legacy comes from a Latin word, *legare*, which means to appoint by law, leave by will. It has the same origin as the word legal.

What are you going to leave behind? To whom are you going to leave anything behind after you're gone? How are you going to leave your estate? When are you going to begin transferring your assets?

When all is said and done, it is all about doing what is right. What we do while we are alive and well and of a sound mind, or what we do even after we are gone, depends on how righteous we are before God and man and family and friends.

Most people really do want an equitable dissolution of their estate for those in their immediate family. The greatest legacy of all is to leave that which says to those we care about the most, You Are Loved, Too.

"Children teach us a whole lot if we let them."

THE MOONA

"Look Mommy! Look! Look up there. There's the moona! There's the moona!" the tiny little boy exclaimed over and over to his mommy as he was leaving Chuck E. Cheese's restaurant. "There's the moona."

Sure enough, he made such a point about the moona being in the sky I looked up along with several other people, and we saw a very clear, distinct quarter moon. As he was being ushered away by his mommy I caught her fading words, "Barry has always called the moon, moona."

Children can express themselves in very deep philosophy sometimes, and even great maturity sliced between their little minds of childhood. This child could not have been more than three years old. He didn't look two feet tall. But he unquestionably and emphatically knew where the moon was. And to him, maybe not to the rest of the whole world, he knew its name—it was the moona.

He got my attention, he got his mommy's attention, and he got a lot of other people's attention that there is a moona in this universe, and it shines brightly sometimes at night, and it's even got a name to it, moona.

As I walked on to my car I thought about so many people in this world who are so busy with life's stresses. We are trying to cope with all of life's mountains and forget just what a wonderful world God has made for us. But not this little child, not Barry. He knows it's up there. He may not understand all about creation and all of the deep philosophy behind evolution, but no one can fool him about his moona.

It would be interesting to sit down with this child and get some other unique names about our world. I wonder what he calls bad people, you know—criminals. I wonder how he labels food, like a hot dog or a hamburger. And I really wonder how he says Jesus when he refers to that perfect man who walked up a hill and gave his life for the sins of the world. If the name rhymes with moona, it's Jeesa. Who knows?

Children teach us a whole lot if we will let them. When I went back inside to see my five-year-old grandson open all his presents, a little boy asked if he could go and play. "No! No!" he was told, "Davin's got to open up all his presents first."

"Oh! No! I'll never get to play," the child cried, "It'll take years for him to open up all his presents."

What a picture of you and me! In our Western, modern thought, we all want it now, today. If it can't be by microwave, it's too long of a wait. All too often we get caught up in the attitude, "It'll take years before we are successful or get the house of our dreams or drive the car we always wanted or find the mate we want to live with or land the job we've prayed for."

See how smart children are? One has taught us how to coin a new name for the Moon. And the other has taught us to slow down and be more patient, even though he'd rather have been playing.

Perhaps the greatest scene of all with the Lord upon this earth was when he received those little kids that the disciples tried to shoo away. There was a purpose, for that I believe. He wanted us to see ourselves in the faces of those children. He wanted to remind us that there's a child in all of us. We shouldn't "get too big for our pants." And we should remember that everybody is important down here—even the little people who call the Moon, Moona.

"(the greatest treasure)...it's found in yourself."

TREASURES WE CAN TOUCH

I just <u>thought</u> I knew my mother. Please hold this thought as you read this and you will understand later. City alleys and downtown parking garages are two places I simply do not like and try to avoid, whether I am in Denver or in another city where I am speaking or visiting. I also do not feel very comfortable when I go into a nursing home or a hospital room. It's funny how you get these feelings of fear and insecurity, but they are as real as the palm of your hand in front of you.

Only recently my mother became critically ill from a heart attack. After her heart surgery and very serious illness, I was able to visit her in her hospital room. "When it rains it pours" is an old proverb that is so very true. Just recently my wife became disabled. I had to arrange my own schedule so I could go to my mother's bedside.

My initial visit was with everyone: my mother and my dad and brothers and other relatives. However, before I caught a plane back to the Mile High City I went by to visit with Mother for a lengthy time. It's amazing how the Lord gives us such wonderful vistas into His presence when we're not even expecting it.

No, I do not like hospital rooms. I've had my own fair share of hospital stays over the years from sicknesses and surgeries. But this night, things changed for me. I went to visit my mother be-cause I was on a mission to give to her comfort, consolation, and as many encouragements as I possibly could.

It did not work this way, however. I became the one who was the receiver, not the giver. I hate to admit this in one way, but in an-other way I do not. This had to be the most precious and tender moment I have ever spent with my own mother, and I am now fifty-eight years old. It was as if we had come full circle, too. Because she was the person I first had a serious talk with about how to become a Christian and accept Christ as my Lord and Savior. This happened when I was a child and only nine years of age.

As I sat for several hours and reminisced with mother I just <u>thought</u> I knew my mother. After her eighty years upon this earth, it dawned upon me that she had graduated to a higher level of spirituality and maturity and wisdom I never knew before. She talked about how people allow things and stuff to take over their lives. She talked about how human behavior ultimately has a price to pay, either for good or for bad. She also talked about my grandfather and how hard a life he had to live.

You would have to know Peggy Johnson, my mother, to appreciate what I am about to say, but she is one of those very few people who fulfills that verse, "Godliness with contentment is great gain." Society and community scenes are things she has never sought or even wanted. Her world has been filled with her love toward her family and friends and her church. The pictures litter the walls of our home there in Orange, Texas, with portraits of her children and grandchildren and her great grandchildren. This has been her biggest trip down here on this planet.

Perhaps the greatest thing about my mother came home to me this night as we visited in a cold, lonely hospital room, and that is her absolute genuineness. She is one of the rarest individuals in this universe when it comes to being herself. She's hardly ever worn much make-up her whole life, or jewelry or fancy stylish clothes; not that this is wrong, of course, but she has graced this stage of life with what millions of people would love to wear, and that is being just who you are.

Most Americans not only lead quiet lives of financial desperation, they also lead empty lives of superficiality and pretense. Somewhere along the way, my mother discovered the most important of all virtues as far as I am concerned, and that is integrity. She has been honest with others, but even more so she has learned to be honest with herself. She truly is just who she is and nothing more.

Since mankind began, he's always been in search of treasures. I am currently reading a new book, *Into Africa*, by Martin Dugard. It's a book about the great missionary, David Livingstone. It relates how this extraordinary man of God risked his life over and over to make discoveries during the 1800s in this unknown land at the time.

Over the centuries mankind has gone into the depths of the sea and into the coldest spots on this earth. He has traveled deep inside the earth itself, and even into space to discover those rare and hidden treasures. But I am totally convinced that the greatest treasure of all is found where everyone can touch it; it's found in yourself. It's right in your heart and mine. God wants our heart more than any other thing we possess. True, He wants us to find Him, but He also wants us to find ourselves. This is why Jesus declared while he was upon this earth, "For where your treasure is, there will your heart be also" (Matthew 6:21).

No, my mother never concerned herself with designer clothes or jewelry, but she has a designer heart. And this night at the hospital I found the greatest treasure of all, and that is just being who you are, not what others want you to be. Most people will live their whole lives trying to be someone they are not. It's like cell phones when they first came out and were so expensive for most of the public to have and use. So a company in California came up with a look-a-like cell phone which people could buy so they could impress people as they drove down the highway. But the truth is, those phones were a façade, just like the people who bought them.

There was nothing that turned Jesus off more than pretense and hypocrisy. Jesus preached against those who lived a double life. He, in fact, lashed out against the religious leaders of his time who taught one thing and practiced another.

My mother reminds me of the tall, slender guy in that marvelous movie, *Savannah Smiles*. If you saw it you will remember at the end of the movie the short chubby guy called Bootsie looks over to his tall, slender counterpart and he asks a question. Do you remember the question? Savannah is being whisked away in a security car along with her mother. The truth is that these two supposedly hard core criminals had taken better care of this child than she was receiving from her dysfunctional parents and socialites.

Bootsie asked, "Do you think they will tell her about us when she gets bigger?" Remember that awesome answer the tall slender guy answered with? He simply said, "To me it doesn't make any difference."

You know, on that premise the whole world would change over night if we could just all catch the power and impact of that one statement. "To me it doesn't make any difference." Why? Because this man knew he had done the right thing by this lovely, lovely little girl. He and Bootsie had treated Savannah with more dignity and love than she had ever received by her highfalutin' parents. He knew they had given her the real attention she had needed since she first came into this world. All hell could break out against him, he could be called the worst thing on this planet one day to this little girl, but in his heart of hearts he knew that he and his little chubby partner had done the right thing by her.

Is it any wonder that he answered, "To me it doesn't make any difference." It's kind of like Twain said one day, "Do what is right and it will gratify most people and astonish the rest."

Somewhere along life's way my saintly mother decided that it just doesn't matter what the world says about her. What she's done on this earth has not been done to impress other people. She knows deep down inside it just doesn't make any difference, because she knows in her heart she's done right by how she's treated her fellow man.

Before I left her bedside my mother reached out her hand and gently said, "Ronnie, let's have prayer." It was then that I knew she was indeed a treasure you can touch. You and I can be touchable treasures, too, by making the right choices for God and for mankind down here in this crazy world. God help us to be ourselves, more importantly, to be more like the man, Jesus Christ, sent by God who brought to each of us eternal life. He is the greatest treasure of all that you and I can touch with one single prayer.

"You are your greatest wealth and asset."

BELLS AND WHISTLES

"....A man's wisdom makes his face to shine, and the boldness of his face shall be changed."

—King Solomon
(Ecclesiastes 8:1b)

She just made a passing comment, "Yeah, we know all about those bells and whistles, don't we?" But it stuck right in my heart. We were looking at a car I'd leased recently through my son-in-law. Nikki, who made this comment, is a friend of the family. Now just hold this thought for a moment please.

Only the other day I walked into a new home which a family had bought. The people had requested an interview, so my associate and I met with them. The family had just moved into Colorado from another state.

After our visit the lady left me with a small gift. She said that she gives them out all the time. She said, in fact, that she had been doing this for years, ever since she had first received one herself.

It was days later when I was going down a Denver highway that I realized my small gift from this lady was right beside me. So I opened up the package and placed the little cassette tape into my car's audio system and started listening.

It's a tape on *The Power of Positive Thinking* by the late Dr. Norman Vincent Peale. As I began to listen to this giant of a man and thinker, I was captivated also by the little lady who gave this to me. There is no telling how many more people to whom she has given this same gift.

My, how we choose to help or to hurt others!

"Ronnie, I order these in mass quantity and just give them away. I've forgotten how many I have dispersed over the years," was her comment to me that day.

Don't you see that we humans have "bells and whistles," too? God ordered them for us when we came into this world, and endowed us with very special "bells and whistles." They're all there, just like on these autos that we drive. Some of us use them and others allow them to corrode over time. What a pity!

Within us is an unlimited potential. It is God given. It is a power beyond our wildest imagination.

We are not robotically made. If we were we would not have choices in this life; everybody would have the same "bells and whistles." But El (The Almighty) has blessed us with many "bells and whistles." For many of us this means eyes to see with, ears to hear with, legs to run and jump with, great voices, and abilities to write and paint and create new ideas and build bridges, roads and tall buildings. Ever just stand back and really look at what man has made with his hands? What tools our hands are themselves! You've got "bells and whistles" you're employing as you clasp that cup of coffee and read this article. Look how you can curl your fingers around that cup handle.

I remember ordering my first Oldsmobile at the dealership that came with cruise control on it. Johnny Christian, a dynamic human being and car salesman in East Texas ordered the car for me. It was on an Oldsmobile Cutlass.

I think I may have had the first cruise control on any vehicle that ever came into that dealership, too. My wife was fearful of it. This was brand new technology at the time. Many people feared that it might get stuck somehow and cause wrecks. In fact, there were quite a few problems early on with cruise control in the early seventies.

But now most cars and trucks come with so many accessories that it takes a thick manual to even read about all the options: from a satellite navigation system to multiple CD systems, from Bose sound to outside temp gauges, from satellite radio with zero commercial interruptions to small TVs and video features, from faxes to computers and more—"Yeah, we all know about those bells and whistles, don't we?"

One of the saddest things I ever read about concerned a couple on Valentine's Day some years ago who were traveling through a wooded area near Belle Chasse, Louisiana. They came upon something white, shimmering in the trees which caught their eyes. As they checked out the scene further, they realized that they had come upon a teenager hanging from a limb on a tree. He had tied a white-knotted bed sheet around his neck.

The stunned couple found a farewell note near the trunk of the tree. It was addressed simply:

To Mom and Dad,

> I never did develop into a real person and I cannot tolerate the false and empty existence I have created...What frustrated me most in the last year was that I had built no ties to family and friends. There was nothing of lasting worth and value. I led a detached existence...I am a bomb of frustration and should never marry and have children. It is safest to defuse the bomb harmlessly now...simply create me as John Doe.

After authorities did everything they could to discover who this youth was, no one responded to the posters which were circulated throughout the country. He was buried both unidentified and unclaimed. Only God knew who he was. What a tragedy!

- Did you know that in this country seventy Americans take their own lives every day?

- Once every minute in this great nation a person attempts suicide.
- In L. A. County, California, more people kill themselves than die in traffic accidents. [1]

I am reminded of Billy Graham telling a story about an officer who went over to a person about to take his life by jumping over the Brooklyn Bridge. After the officer talked with the person for a few minutes, they both jumped over.

Just think of all the "bells and whistles" that go to waste every day in this nation because people forget just how much worth and value they really have. I'm convinced that the greatest waste and loss in our nation is not in energy, ecology, our time, or even ill-spent money. No! It's when human beings lose sight of who they are and why they're even here on this planet.

You are your greatest wealth and asset.

Don't ever forget it either. You and I have at our disposal the greatest, latest, most innovative "bells and whistles" under the sun.

If you could only realize the power within you; all those accessories the Lord has given you are right at your fingertips. You choose to be who you are. You choose to be happy or a grouch. There are all kinds of buttons you have that you can push. You can choose your whole life and attitude. and the lives and attitudes of those around you.

Every day you can set your cruise control on confidence or failure. You can turn on your navigation system and map out a great, efficient day, or follow a map of negativism and pessimism. You can turn on your Bose stereo with a spring in your step, a smile on your face, and joy in your heart, or you can conjure up all those old past feelings of hate and remorse and regrets. "Yeah, we all know about all those bells and whistles, don't we?" Use them.

1. Charles R. Swindoll, *Come Before Winter*. Portland, Oregon: Multnomah Press, 1985.

"Being there, that's what it's all about really."

BEING THERE

It's been years now since my wife Nancy and I lost a beautiful little infant daughter, Janet Elizabeth Johnson, stillborn (nine months). In fact, it will be three decades next year in June. Some things you just don't forget in life. They are like the air you breathe and the steps you take if you are so blessed to be able to walk.

My mind recalls so vividly at times all those people dressed in black waiting for me that day at a cemetery in Orange, Texas. My late father-in-law and I drove for several hours from East Texas with the little girl's body in a pink casket; we placed it in the back seat of my car. Nancy at that time was still in the hospital having undergone a C-section; she was unable to travel.

But Oh! That little band of people at the cemetery dressed for the occasion; they didn't have to say one thing to me. They were just there. In fact, I don't even remember talking to all of them. They were just there with their expressions of love and sympathy and care. Real care, too. Those dark suits and dresses brightened my life because the people who were wearing them cared enough to come to my side in my greatest sorrow.

Something swelled up inside me that day that I have never forgotten. It was that incredible reality that while you're still here and in this land of the living, there are people who do love you and care about you and want you to realize that you are here for a very special purpose. This was a day when all of those people could have been somewhere else: at work, on a trip, shopping, watching their TVs, doing their own thing. But they were there, there with me shedding tears and sorrow on a hot June day in a time of loss.

The Apostle Paul writes about a man who was there for him when he was in a cold, dark dungeon for speaking out about Christ his Lord. His name was Onesiphorus. The Apostle declared, "For he oft refreshed me, and was not ashamed of my chains: but, when he was in Rome, he sought me out very diligently, and found me. The Lord grant unto him that he may find mercy of the Lord in that day: and in how many things he ministered unto me at Ephesus, you know very well,"   -(2 Timothy 1:16-18 KJV).

Being there, that's what it's all about, really. This man, just like the little band of people from my church, the Cove Baptist Church in Orange, Texas, was there. He was there by Paul's side; they were there by my side. What encouragements!

All too often we hear about all the bad things going on in this earth. But what about those people every day who bring smiles to our eyes, inspiration to our lives and love to our hearts?

I looked up that word, refresh, " for he oft 'refreshed' me...," the Apostle wrote. It is the word, *anapsucho* (Greek), *ana* and *psucho* placed together. It means to cool off. This man would go and cool off the Apostle Paul with his presence and encouraging visits. Wow! And Onesiphorus did this consistenly, too, "for he oft...," says the scriptures.

If you look even more closely at the words, *ana* and *psucho* you find that *ana* means "up" and *psucho* means "to breathe gently, voluntarily." Wow! What a marvelous thought! We are always cooled off when we get that second wind, when we are filled with that exhilaration from a renewed breath of fresh air. It's like cool water to a parched tongue.

"Here Paul." Can't you just hear Onesiphorus sort of whisper, "Here, take a swig of this grape juice I brought you; and there in that pouch is some cool water from our well, too."

And Paul didn't forget either. You don't forget people in life who refresh you. You just don't forget them, do you?

This is why we are all the better because someone takes the time to keep us company and cool us off day by day. Remember, "I will never leave you nor forsake you." His Spirit is with you and me everyday. When we're crying and when we're laughing, when we're working and when we're playing, when we're driving and when we're resting, the Dove of heaven and the Breath of life, the Holy Spirit, the Spirit of Christ is there cooling us off.

I honestly can't remember who was there that day, not everyone. My dad, my mother and my pastor, my father-in-law, some family members, and a host of people from my home church—but it doesn't matter. God knows each of them. He knows who took time that day to refresh the soul of an anxious, restless, broken heart of a young minister.

Every time I go back home now I always go to Janet's little grave site. And every time I stand there I reflect back upon that small band of church people, clad in black, who were there for me in one of the saddest days of my entire life upon this planet. And I thank God for how they cooled me off that dark, dreary day. How? By just being there. I hope and pray to God that one day someone will remember me, too, for just being there for them in their crisis. Their presence spoke more words than any language could have ever expressed. Why? How? Being there.

"Losing is reality."

LOSING

He was a tall, lanky Texan who went by the name of Coolie. In today's world he'd really be in, you know, he'd be cool with a name like this. Coolie, or PaPa as we would call him, was a circuit-riding Baptist preacher. He owned at one time several hundred acres of farm and ranch land in East Texas, or as we always said, "up in East Texas." The reason it was "up" to us is because after we all left the farm we moved to the coast of Southeast Texas, which in some places is below sea level.

Coolie was a very unique individual. For one thing, he couldn't read anything but the Bible. This, for some reason, was not the most uncommon thing in the world because I have heard of a few other people from earlier centuries who could do the same. Whether it was divine intervention or what, I can't say—I would like to think so.

Another unique thing about PaPa Coolie was his unique ability to pray. When he prayed he had a way of taking everybody in his presence right to the throne of heaven and to the heart of God. In church he would stand as they used to do, when called upon to pray. People who are still alive remember this man and his moving, spiritual prayers that he so passionately voiced to the Lord. His prayers were so genuine and poignant that people just haven't forgotten; they may have forgotten the sermon, but not Coolie's praying.

Coolie, however, experienced life how it really is and not how Hollywood makes it to be so often, you know, "and they lived happily together thereafter." He lost more than half of his farm and ranch during the Great Depression. It was during this period of time that he also lost his loving wife, Eva. And he lost a son on top of this because she contracted measles during her pregnancy. They were both buried together, mother and child.

Coolie had five boys and two daughters at this time to raise on his own. Can you imagine going through the Great Depression and suddenly becoming a single-parent family with seven hungry mouths to feed? Wow! He must have felt like Job at this time.

It is so interesting to me how we get in our minds down here, one, that we are going to live forever, and two, life is going to be all sweet and rosy. Dr. Charles Swindoll once shared in a radio program how his daughter wrote them at home; she had gone away to college. The gist of the message in the card was, "Dear Mom and Dad, I hate to tell you this but I am pregnant, I have flunked out of school, I'm afraid I'm going to have to move back in with you guys, I wrecked my car (it was just a bunch of negative stuff like this as I remember that she included). On and on, her bad luck was listed on the card.

Dr. Swindoll said that he turned the card over after almost falling out his chair and the card said, "Just kidding, Mom and Dad. I love you. April Fool!"

I shall never forget sharing this with my friend, the prophet. He said, "You know Ron, I know that Swindoll meant that as something kind of cute to his listeners on the air, but that's really more true of how life really is than not."

Losing. This is life. We have so many people trying to teach us otherwise. But losing is reality. Especially here in the West, people spend millions and millions of dollars on self-help books to help them have a winning spirit and a positive attitude. And this is good. But life has never been meant to live without losing. It is a part of the very fabric of our being, and of nature. I'm convinced after all these years that it's not the losing that really counts anyway, but it's how we react and respond to those losing situations that make the big difference.

But I do believe that if we realize that in life we are either headed into a storm, or we're going to be right in the middle of a storm, or thank God we've just come out of a storm, we're much stronger in dealing with reality rather than superficiality. Life is much more a tragedy than it is a triumph. We are going to lose loved ones. We are going to lose friends. We are going to lose our job at one time or another in life. We are going to lose money in the stock market. We are going to lose our health eventually as we age. This is life, what's on the front of that card, not what's on the back—April Fool!

Coolie eventually lost his second wife. Then he lost his health and was bedridden for a number of years. I used to roll his cigarettes for him, bring him meals, help bathe him, feed him, clothe him, and clean him. Finally he lost his life; he died in his seventies.

I remember reading about an Olympic runner in the sixties who lost a marathon race in his homeland in Japan. His name was Kokichi Tsuburaya. Before his own countrymen in the 1964 Tokyo Games he knew he would probably not win first place, but he had expected to win second. As he and a British runner, Ben Heatley, entered the great coliseum, the young Japanese runner was way ahead. But right before the Emperor and 80,000 spectators, he allowed the British runner to come from behind and defeat him. He lost the coveted silver medal he wanted so badly to win.

Later on, when this young Japanese runner was training for the Mexico City Olympics, he took his own life. Losing was just too much for him to bear any longer. The suicide note which was found by his side simply read, "I cannot run anymore."

I can honestly say that as a Christian I am so thankful that no matter what I lose here I know I have gained there. Christ taught us, "In the world you will have troubles (losses: divorce, death, disability and difficulties), but be happy because I have overcome this place down here" (St. John 16:33 RJV). This is my version, more or less.

On the other side awaits our daughter and family and dear friends. For the true believer our loss here means our gain over there (heaven). Or, the way the Apostle Paul put it, "For to me to live is Christ, and to die is gain [far better]" (Philippians 1:21 KJV).

In my office in Denver, I have drawn a portrait of both Jared Wright Johnson, my great grandfather, and Coolie Johnson, my grandfather. I see them both every day. And I am reminded of the rich heritage they have left behind to my father and his family, and for myself and my own family. People often ask, "Who are those people hanging there on the wall?"

I have decided now, after all these years, that losing is life's way of gaining if you will allow it, and learn from your losses. Losses can be great burdens of guilt and despair, or they can become great blessings of gifts and determination. Someone told me that a father and mother's education really begins after they are gone. It's like we have to lose in order to gain.

Only recently my associate and I learned a valuable lesson from a man whom we more or less lost a sale to. But we met with him and learned what made him go in a different direction. What a difference that has made in our practice! I cannot tell you how valuable a lesson we both learned from this person. Losing doesn't have to be losing; losing can be gaining if we let it—if we study it.

I like to think that PaPa Coolie learned in the end just how valuable losing really is. His favorite saying was, "This world is just one big problem." There are two ways we can look at this: one, it really is just one big problem: headaches, flat tires, hangnails, toothaches, backaches, dead batteries and burnt toast; and two, I know it's one big problem I know what I'm up against, but with God on my side I don't care what I face today, I know I have Someone with me all the way.

What about you? Do you feel like you're losing all the time? There's hope for all of us. PaPa Coolie used to say, "You can't ever tell the luck of a lousy calf." That's right, too. Sometimes the runt of the litter or the most straggly calf on the range will one day become the prized steer.

I believe we must learn from our losses, and let them become pluses. With God's help anything is possible. All things are possible, everything is possible with El's insurmountable strength in your life.

"You have a jingle about you. You just do."

I MISS HIS JINGLE

Our son always fell on the floor with Pugsley when he came home. Pugsley, our Boston terrier, would jump around and try to lick Jason's face. And, of course, Jason would cover his face with his hands. But inevitably Jason's broad shoulders and big, six foot body would find a place on the floor for that favorite attention that he would always get from a dog who loved him and whom he loved as well.

It's really only been days since I had to make that sad walk to "put Pugs down." He was approximately thirteen years of age at his death. Pugsley was one of those animals that just got under your skin, even if you didn't like animals or pets. I would actually take him into the office each day and everyone treated him like a king. He had that muted colored face with half black and half white that gave him a very distinct look as a Boston terrier.

For those of you who have lost a really close, loving and unique kind of pet, you will understand just how great the loss can be. Those little animals have a personality all their own. They teach us a lot about how people should be treated, and how we want to be treated as well.

Only recently Jason made a passing comment one day when we were reflecting on all the good times with Pugs. He said, "You know, I miss his jingle." Because of the dog tag and his identity on his collar, two little pieces of metal would jingle when he moved. So when we came in the house or heard him going to get a drink, or if he was playing around, that most distinct jingle could be heard.

I started thinking about Jason's comment and I have not been able to get it out of my mind. Why? Because in reality we all have a jingle. People just recognize us by our attitude, our demeanor, and our disposition. Crabby or cool, snooty or soothing, sneaky or suave, snobbish or sensible, critical or caring, distrustful or delightful, silly or sincere, shaky or stable, believe me, you and I are known for one of the two in most cases. People may not be honest enough to level with us, but people in their own private discussions share either the hurt and sorrow over such people or the happiness and joy. You have a jingle about you, you just do.

In the scriptures we are taught that we are known by our fruit which we bear. Same truth! You and I can hide our behavior just so long. The real stuff in all of us eventually surfaces; it just can't be hid. Even children pick up on our jingle. They tell you, too. What a great opportunity to afford each of us in this life - to spread the jingle of hope and cheer, of assurance and uplifting thoughts to those who so desperately need it.

Pugsley was rarely ever a problem to us. I often told people, "He looks vicious, but you'll bite him long before he'll bite you. He was one of those exceptionally mature little dogs. He was more like a child than a pet at times, a really good child, too. His jingle was refreshing. Don't you wish you could say that about everybody you know? He brought us laughter and uplifting feelings. Don't you wish you could say that about everybody? He made us feel good about ourselves because he was around. Don't you wish you could say that about everybody you know?

But don't be surprised if people act like people: rude, egotistical, smart alecks, arrogant and overbearing. Sad to say, but some people's jingle makes us all wince and cringe when they walk in the door, right? They've disappointed us enough that we just know the very scent of their jingle stinks.

No wonder the great mind William James declared, "You can alter the way you live by changing the attitude of your mind." You can, too, if you're willing to seek help. Whether it is from a professional, a small group setting, at church, through prayer, or whatever it takes, you can alter your own life if you choose to change that attitude. No one else can make this move for you. No one! You must decide that you want a change.

What a jingle the Lord, the Master had when he walked this old earth! If we could only go back in time. Those soldiers sent out by religious leaders who returned to give a report on the man they were supposed to arrest cried, "No one ever spoke the way this man does." They were so enthralled by Christ's compassionate words and captivating message that they could not even think of arresting such a person. "For what?" they must have thought to themselves. "This guy isn't a criminal; this is a gentle, caring person pointing people to God and to righteousness."

How people must have missed the Lord's jingle after he left this world! His incredible jingle, his character and touching life! Yes, when someone is gone whom we've loved, when their life ends before our lives, their jingle goes, too. Certainly a pet is a far cry from a human being much less the Savior of the world, but once life is over, the jingle is silenced, too. Their memory lingers with us, but that jingle is over. No wonder the Lord sent his comforting Spirit to lead and guide us by his incessant presence (jingle).

By God's grace and help let us all remember just how significant our jingle is to those who know us and love us so much. Be a bright, shining light while you can, where you are, while you have the time. We must be careful to not get too used to a person's jingle and take them for granted because life can end so soon.

Only recently Nancy and I lost a lady who has been a unique friend to us for over thirty years. At a church I pastored many years ago the church leaders wanted to get rid of her because she worked at a bar at night. I refused their request. Ever since then Viola Moore has remembered us at Christmas time and on special occasions. Of all the thousands of people Nancy and I met and pastored over our lifetime in ministry, no one, not a single person or church, ever remembered us like she did. Her jingle was a resounding one! Right up until her death she was still giving herself (her jingle) to the aged and the dying.

Yes, I can still hear Pugsley's jingle, too. I'm glad I gave so much to a little creature down here while I had the opportunity. I just hope my own jingle will encourage your heart today with these words of ink on paper before your eyes. Keep your jingle going! The world definitely needs more jingling and joy today.

I like the way the great Apostle coached his young minister friend:

> But you (Timothy) - keep your eye on what you're doing; accept the hard times along with the good; keep the Message alive; do a thorough job as God's servant (2 Timothy 4:5 TMV).

Paul was declaring to him "Keep the Message (the Good News Jingle) alive." That's it! Keep the most important jingle of all loud and clear to the world around you.

"...things will change for you."

JUST A LITTLE WHILE LONGER

Some time ago, I was at an office. A lady I met recently expressed to me that she was really going through a lot. And in passing she expressed, "It's hard what the Lord is allowing me to go through, but I know He's told me, 'Just a little while longer.'"

Boy, how God speaks to us through his servants. This lady is a true Christian, you can just tell. She walks with God. She talks to Him and He talks to her. And it is evident.

"Just a little while longer," our heavenly Father often advises us. Don't get too low and too upset and too discouraged, because things will change for you.

God's comforts and assurances are always there for us. When He speaks to us like He did to me through this little lady, you will know. God doesn't speak just to be speaking. When He talks, you can be sure a message is on the way.

Maybe your heart is broken right now. Maybe you're going through a real crisis or adversity. Perhaps you feel there's no way out this time. Well, I am writing you now just like this lady spoke to me to say what God led her to say. As difficult and trying as your experience is, just remember it's "just a little while longer."

You may think it's over for you. You may feel that you're at the end of a shabby, worn-out rope, but "just a little while longer" and you'll make it through the midnight storm. Remember that verse of scripture, "Weeping may endure for a night, but joy comes in the morning" (Psalm 30:5 KJV). That's what the Lord is really saying to us, "just a little while longer." No wonder this was my late mother-in-law's favorite verse in the whole Bible.

Then it will be over, finished. The tears will go. The agony will vanish. The pain will end, the dark clouds will turn to sunshine, and the fears of hopelessness will be over. Wow! What a God we serve! He even reminds us that our trials, no matter how horrible and hurtful they really are— "just a little while longer," and then He will carry us through that long lonely valley. What assurance! There's hope after all. I will get through this. Surely the Psalmist was expressing this same thought when he said, "Yea, though I walk through the valley of the shadow of death…"

He did not stay in that dark valley. The Lord brought him through it. Yes, he went through it, but just a little while longer and he found himself upon another mountain beholding the vast horizon before him. Just imagine as the sun was setting with brilliant colors before him and the glow of heaven itself sat upon the earth. David must have thought of those incredible words the Lord breathed upon his heart, "Yea, though I walk through the valley of the shadow of death…" And now he could say, "That valley is behind me, it's gone! It's over forever! Thank God!"

> Just a little while longer
> And I just know I'll get through
> It may seem like a million years
> But I know He'll take care of me and you

Your future depends upon your day by day faith. What you think is of great consequence. Keep your mind fresh with good, healthy reading material. People who've visited our home say they love the positive spiritual literature which is throughout each room of our home; especially in our bathrooms.

God is with you in the "just a little while longer" experiences you must go through. He is there with you, every second , every minute, every hour of every day. And trust him - with His greatest presence and power - it really is "just a little while longer."

"In the shadow of an "it" there really is a difference."

THAT IT

Just once in a great while after tons and tons of hard work and tireless hours do we ascend to those higher levels of expertise and noble victories and august experiences of mastery. Then comes that inexplicable phenomenon called "it." No kidding! It's as real as the palm of your hand in front of you.

The "it" I am talking about is as real as the air you breathe and the ground under your feet. You really don't have to be a rocket scientist to see this or realize the authenticity of a true "it."

An "it" just is. Some people are endowed with such extraordinary gifts and talents that as an "it" they really do not have to muster near the energy a person who is not an "it." However, there are those people who work so hard at their skills and are so determined to aspire to those levels of expertise and sheer wonderment that they excel into the "it" category.

Mastery is a very commanding thing. We are drawn to mastery of a skill or talent. The great violinist, the incredible soloist, the remarkable athlete, the talented gymnast, the awesome artist, the sensational pianist, the wise sculptor, and the marvelous teacher, draw us to them and their rare abilities. They bring us to such emotions and tears of ecstasy. "How can this be?" We ask.

In the shadow of an "it" there really is a difference. No way to explain it. It just exists. It's just there. It is as real as the sun that beats upon our heads on a mid-August day.

Whether a person, a band, a team, an orchestra, a movie, a book, a building, a story, an animal, a scenic view, a rare car or invention, or carving, the "it" is just there staring us in the face. And it is a cut above anything else we've ever seen or experienced.

What a privilege it is! What a privilege you and I have had by being in the shadow of some extraordinary "its" over the past years.

"There is an unbelieveable freedom when you accept who you really are."

PSEUDOPHANTASTICA

"**R**on," the Prophet asked me several years ago, "did you really listen to those closing lines of the supposedly bad guys in the movie, *Savannah Smiles?*'"

The Prophet, for those of you who are new readers of mine, is a man named Joe who lives alone in the woods of Southeast Texas. Over many years now he has helped me many times catch a clearer and more concise view and understanding of mankind and of God and His glorious majesty. Nothing syrupy about him or his religion; he's one of the most genuine and real down-to-earth Christians I know who is left on this planet. But as a modern-day prophet, most believers would never go with his old-fashioned beliefs and convictions.

"No Joe," I explained, "I don't even know what you're talking about."

Joe paused and then said, "Well, I'm not trying to be mean, but I'm not going to tell you. You'll have to check it out and listen for yourself and then we'll discuss the meaning, OK?"

I agreed, and of course, I went to the nearest video place and watched this movie that same evening. Do you remember what they said?

The chubby guy, Bootsie, asked the tall, lanky guy, "I wonder what they'll tell her about us when she gets bigger?"

The tall, lanky guy replied with great confidence and assurance in his heart, "It doesn't make any difference to me."

Although both the mother and the father of this child had actually been ignoring Savannah, these two supposedly bad guys found themselves in custody of one of the most beautiful little neglected girls in this world. In the end they were apprehended for child abduction, but in reality both Savannah and these two men had bonded in life more deeply than she ever had with her high-society parents.

Those words, "It doesn't make any difference to me," ring loud and clear within my heart every so often. The Prophet knew I would go and check this movie out. And he knew what kind of a message I needed to hear. I can truthfully say that it didn't matter to me if no one else in this universe heard his message. I did, and I needed it and still do to this day.

Joe never had to discuss it with me after that. He knew I would get it - and boy did I get it! I am a very visual person if I may be so totally honest and personal with you. Transparent as well. I am easily impressed with people. And I am often tempted to want to impress people myself. I can't speak for you or for anyone else, only for myself; I have always battled trying to be just myself. My dad has often told me over the years, "Ronnie, when you're in the company of influential and sophisticated people and you feel a little over your head, just always be yourself and you'll be OK."

It's easily said, but rarely done by most of us. We all want success. We all want to aspire. We all want to win; deep, deep down within each of us is an incessant desire to win—never to lose. This is why I believe the great coach, Vince Lombardi, asked once, "Why keep score if you don't want to win?" Good question.

But you know, ever since the Prophet pointed this out to me in this movie I can truthfully say that the Lord has convicted me about being just who I am. It is appalling, but true and sad, that millions of people go to their own graves always living in a world of pretense, always trying to be someone they're not.

There is unbelievable freedom when you accept who you really are. Who you really are not. Who you really never will be and never even hope to be. In fact, you will find that other people will even envy you when you become totally honest with yourself and who you are.

The very thing I am talking about right now is what took the life of our Savior and Christ—He was just who He said He was, and the people of His day would not accept Him. Many still do not to this day. He tried to explain that His Father had sent Him on the mission to save this world from their sins, but the world rejected that. Rejected Him, too.

G. K. Chesterton once said, "There was only one thing certain about man—that man is not what he was meant to be."

In the medical world, it's often called pseudophantastica. This is the person who wants Savannah to grow up thinking they're something they really aren't - like her parents in this movie. Pseudophantastica is that person who loves the fantastic account of his or her victories and successes, which are really a lie. Sadly enough they begin to believe they're somebody they're not.

What an encumbrance to carry around in your heart all your life! Wow! What freedom there really is when you and I can say, it doesn't make any difference who we are. The tall, lanky man just knew in his heart what he had done was right by this child and what was in her best interest.

Woa, what freedom! What freedom from pretense! No facade! No superficial thought! No lie! Just plain old me. "It doesn't make any difference." No, it doesn't when you're just who you are.

"You are a treasure."

PEOPLE, YOU ARE ONE

Never forget just how unique you really are. No one else has your smile, or voice, or personality. Out of billions of creatures who walk this green earth, there is only one you. God made you in His image. You have a body, mind, and soul. Everything about you is important both to this human race and to God.

Think about it, out of all the nations and peoples and languages and cultures and continents on this globe, there is only one you. Your thoughts and gifts and talents and creative ideas and achievements are all, just yours. They are completely and totally yours.

Every piece of art, every song you've written, every poem, every sculpture, every design and every dress you made or quilt you've sewn is yours. Every book you've written or article you've penned is yours. You are a treasure. You are God's gift to us all.

All of us with our twenty-four vertebrae, our twelve pairs of ribs, our 500 muscles or more, our twelve pairs of cranial nerves and thirty-one pairs of spinal nerves and how many more anatomy parts make us all very special to our Creator. From the crown of your head to the soles of your feet, you are a walking treasure with the breath of life within you. Your value to others is inestimable.

This is why it hurts so deeply when a family member says something hurtful to you. You have no earthly idea of how valuable you are to the human society in which you live. You can say one word and either make or break a person's day. Your influence and inspiration to those who know you are so far reaching that no one could ever place a price upon such support and encouragement.

As a person you have a profound meaning and value to others.

When a life is snuffed out suddenly it is no wonder no one really knows how to react. You are so taken by the memory and the influence of such a person that only tears can write your sorrow and hurt.

It is beyond me how anyone can cut off relations with a loved one or a former friend or business associate, but we all do, don't we? Why? You and I don't want to be disappointed again either by a lie or a misunderstanding.

You and I have a very brief time upon this earth to do all we can where we are with our God given abilities, while there is time. If you wreck your car you can get another one. Stain a garment, you can buy another. Have a house burn down, you can build another. Lose a ring or watch or pocket knife, you can purchase another. If you break a lovely vase or expensive piece of china, you can re-place it with another. But not a human life. You cannot replace people.

This past year a young lady referred people to work with me in my business. When I see this young lady or think about her I think about just how valuable these people have become to me and my business and to the clientele that I am so thankful to work for and with. How do you appraise such a person and her referrals?

You appraise homes and cars and jewelry and stuff, but just how do you appraise a human life? There is absolutely no one else in this universe or in any other universe who is like you. Even the most perfect twins are still light years apart in every way. Once you get to know twins or triplets you discover that they are so incredibly different in every way.

Everything you do and say and write and create and draw and paint and build and put together is you. I have called people or they have called me and it has been years since we made contact; yet they will know my voice right away. How astounding!

The human brain with its 3 to 5 billion cells is by far the most advanced computer and design under this sun. What's going on between the human ears is a system that we are only beginning to understand; it is a marvel beyond marvels. Imagine the skyscrapers that began in someone's brain. What about these giant airplanes and super charged cars and ocean liners and computers and super highways that began in a brain? You are unique. Your mind makes you so.

Imagine, too, out of all the many peoples who have come and gone in life from one generation to another— millions, billions—not one single person is the same. Different hair and noses and ears and teeth and feet and cheeks and lips and eyes and foreheads and necks and arms and legs - all are different. What a marvel! You being you. Me being me. You not being me. And me not being you.

God has fashioned every one of us differently, so differently and so uniquely. You are truly a walking treasure upon this earth for a very distinct purpose. Your potential and the power you possess to accomplish things are unlimited. Within you are more resources than all the rivers and mountains of this world than all the stars that shine and all the trees that spiral toward heaven. Within that beating heart that brings oxygen to your brain exists incomparable passions to change other hearts and bring hope to empty lives.

Yes, you are just one person on this planet. But oh! How important you really are! Your worth will never be exhausted. The print you leave here will touch lives for eternity. No wonder the Lord asked, "What should it profit a man if he gained the whole world and lost his own soul?" Think about it. Christ was telling you in these words just how much you are worth. You are priceless to Him. You are to me. You are to everyone. You are even to yourself. And there is only one you.

"We all get into these deep, deep ruts in life."

WARPED WAYS

"**R**on," she said with a very strong affirmation, "I think I am going to change things in my life. I am going to change where I am going to church, and some other functions I attend and look for some new thinking."

She paused awhile and then continued with what appeared even more new energy. "I think, Ronnie, you can get stale if you just stay with the same group of people too long and keep listening to the same ideas and the same old way of thinking." Another long pause, "Do you think I'm wrong?"

"Well, no I don't," I responded with a bit of surprise from her decision. It just didn't seem like her for some reason. "No, I don't. In fact, you're inspiring me to think about what you're thinking."

As I drove home at the end of the day, I could not get this eighty-year-old lady and what she had said off my mind. Goodness, she is so right, so very, very right; most people just don't even think about it, I guess. Well, I'm sure they don't. What warped ways we all get into and never come to this conclusion.

True, there is something about "staying," something about tradition and drawing strength from longtime relationships, but we all need a refreshing voice and idea now and then. And when ways become so warped, so stale and turbid, it's time for change.

Candy, my wife's sister, has always seemed to lead in the way of innovative ideas and introducing us to new things which are happening. She is one of those very creative, gifted and talented human beings who always comes up with fresh ideas. For years now, when I call or Nancy calls to talk to her, I always ask Candy what new thing she's into.

Every day we observe a lovely stained glass masterpiece. It is in the living room of our home. It hangs in the front of a big window and lets the sunrays filter beautiful colors into our house every day. Candy made this years ago, one of the many things she has tackled: from pottery to stain glass, from charcoal drawings to art work, I think she's tried it all.

When we moved to Colorado in the late eighties Candy said to me something that has never left me. She said, "Ronnie, you are going to grow so much there I think. You'll learn new ideas, meet brand new people and experience all kinds of new ways—you're gonna grow a lot; I just know this will be the case."

Wow, was Candy right! Moving from Texas to Colorado has changed my whole life; it's changed my family's life, too. Grow? Yes. New ways? Yes. Brand new people, friends? Yes. From one state to another has been like another brand new world, no comparison really.

Why do we accept those warped ways, do you think? Because we all do. We all get in those deep, deep ruts in life. And the deeper they get, the more difficult it is to maneuver, turn and even get out of the ruts.

I remember attending a funeral in East Texas a number of years ago. A fresh rain had fallen and the lead car in the procession made a wrong turn. All of the cars got stuck in muddy red dirt that day because we drove off the paved road. It was a mess to say the least! It turned into a clay-like road. Cars spun their tires, motors raced loudly, and plumes of smoke filled the air. We were all trying our best to stay in the ruts just long enough to get back to the paved road.

What a picture of people's ways and thinking! All too often we just stay in those ruts and go nowhere. We stay there spinning in our thinking, racing our hearts and letting steam off just like those cars.

When the Lord was upon the earth those scribes and Pharisees came to him and asked him why in the world were his disciples not washing their hands before they ate bread. Why were they breaking the tradition of their fathers?

The Lord explained to them that their lip service and traditional, warped ways were keeping them from God, not getting them to God. After the Lord spoke to these warped-minded religious leaders, his disciples came to him. They wanted to know if the Lord realized that he had offended them.

The Lord explained to his disciples that one, they had no spiritual roots with God, and two, they were the blind leading the blind, headed for a ditch (ruts) in which they were going to fall into.

The Lord also made one of the most profound statements I think in his entire ministry. He said, "Let them alone" (St. Matthew 15:14 KJV).

Was this what this little lady was saying to me? I need to get away from that old way of thinking. I need to remove myself from the same old stale ideas and philosophy I get week after week from the same resources. Am I wrong to want something better for myself? Am I wrong to want to remove myself from the same old people with the same old mindset and the same old beliefs and opinions that I've been listening to for years and years?

"Let them alone." Wow! What a statement! Just let them alone, you make sure that you go on to bigger and better and richer and newer ideas and ways of thought and lifestyles. Get yourself away from that same old thinking. Move on... you'll see the newer waters aren't so bad after all.

How really sad that some people become so embedded in the circle of their thoughts and lifestyles, going around and around in the same old tracks. Just like the children of Israel who wandered for forty years in the same wilderness, when they were just minutes away from the Promised Land. That's sad! But this can be a picture of all of us if we are not careful.

I like what the Apostle Paul says in his writing to the Corinthian church. If a person is "in Christ, he is a new creature: old things are passed away; behold all things are new" (Corinthians 5:77 KJV).

Remember, "if you're green you grow, but if you're ripe you'll rot."

There are new friends to be made all around us. There are new ideas to be found, new programs to learn about, brand new experiences to be experienced, and new horizons to discover that we never thought even existed. I challenge you as I challenge myself to lift up your head and your heart, and dream new dreams and aspire to the new vistas staring us in the face. With God's help all things are possible and not even the sun's the limit for what we can accomplish for Christ, for humanity, and for ourselves.

This doesn't mean we shun those timeless spiritual principles and spiritual laws that bring us closer to God and make us more God-conscious. What this little lady said to me was that I must guard against that warped way of thinking that inhibits our spiritual growth and brings stagnation to our ability to learn new ideas. And these can be life-changing both for us and for others. Just as the scriptures teach us, "Lift up your heads..." Look around you. What incredibly marvelous opportunities stand before us everyday. God help you and me to take advantage of them while we can.

"He (God) is our life coach."

THROUGH THE EYES OF THE PROPHET

"Joe," I asked, "Why was Cotton so great? Why was it that he won so many state championships in high school basketball as a coach? Other coaches have had the same passion, work just as hard and have wanted to win just as bad, but many never even win a district championship, much less a state championship? Why is this do you think?"

"Ron, he was a genius," Joe quickly retorted.

"A genius?" I asked.

"Yes, a genius. Cotton was like many people who are just a hair-line different from being an idiot and a genius, and he was a genius." Joe continued. "That's why he won so many championships. He could see things happening on the court before anyone else even thought about it."

I thought aloud, "You mean like Tiger Woods or Larry Bird or Babe Ruth or Michael Jordon...Cotton was born with this; it was God-given?"

"Yes," the prophet explained. "Now this doesn't mean they haven't fine tuned what they have been endowed with. We don't want to take away from them what they've done. But Ron, Cotton was an absolute genius. I remember years ago he suited up a real tall boy for Buna (small Southeast Texas town where Cotton coached). He was about 6'6". Back then that was tall, too. He did this just to get the tip for each quarter. After they got the tip he would seat the boy on the bench, but he knew that would mean eight points each game he'd have in the bag. The young man really wasn't much of a basketball player, but Cotton saw that he could jump real high. Ron, that's just the way Cotton thought."

"Well, Joe, I just never thought about it that way, but it makes sense. It actually bothers me sometimes when I think about Cotton that he was so successful, such a winner—and you know other coaches try so hard and spend the same number of hours, maybe even more, but they don't win that many championships. I remember people saying before Cotton and his team would leave Austin, Texas they would book the same rooms again a year in advance for the next state championship (they just knew they'd be back the next year). But now I think I know why; what you say makes a lot more sense to me. He really was a genius."

"Well, remember now, Ronnie," the prophet made his point clearly. "Cotton was a genius, but he sacrificed the time and energy to develop what he already had. A lot of coaches are developing what they have, too, but they ain't geniuses."

Joe just has a way of saying it. "Cotton Robinson could look out across a court and he could just envision what was going to happen before it would even occur. Remember that Hillin boy?"

"Yeah! I went to college with him. I played against him in high school, too. He was really good."

"There was one particular spot just to the left of the free throw line that was his territory," the prophet reminisced more. "He knew it like the back of his hand. And he was deadly from there, too. He seldom missed a shot there. Well, that's the way Cotton coached, Ronnie. He had each player excelling in what the player did best. That's even more reason why he was such a genius at coaching. He had every player doing what he did best in the position where he played."

"Ron, I'm not so sure the players he coached, or the coaches he went up against ever understood altogether what he was even doing at the time. Cotton was that well advanced in coaching at the time; he was definitely ahead of his time. He was just that smart."

Today, as people pass through Buna, Texas, there is a monument to both Cotton Robinson and R. C. Hyden, a very successful girls' basketball coach as well. Some years ago I stopped there and read about both these great coaches.

As you view this monument, Hyden is pictured to the left and M. N. "Cotton" Robinson is pictured to the right. Below is Cotton's incredible record of 538 wins and 98 losses and seven state championships. Hyden had won four state championships himself.

Below both of them is etched:

Buna, Texas
Home of Eleven State Championships
1955 Through 1963

Wow! That really says it all, doesn't it? Yet, Cotton was such a simple man in so many ways. He wore a crew cut. He dressed very modestly. He drove an average car. He actually seemed to be a very quiet, private man. But in the days of my high school years he was a Vince Lombardi on the high school basketball court. Honestly, he was like a god to all us kids and coaches who knew him. Other coaches studied him night and day to try to find out his secrets to such success.

He was exactly like the prophet said, "A genius."

You know, we all wonder sometimes why things are the way they are and why people are the way they are. I learned a lot from what the prophet taught me this day about Cotton. I'm glad I asked him, because I had no idea he was such a gifted man with high intelligence. I am convinced that there is a reason and purpose for everything; we just often do not understand the underlying reasons and answers.

Remember when Moses asked the Lord, "Who shall I say that has sent me?"

And the Lord told him, "Tell them (the Egyptians) I Am that I Am has sent you." When we think about it God is just that. He is just who He is and nothing more and nothing less. He doesn't have to impress anyone: name brand clothes, fancy car, big house, or Rolex watch—He's just who He is: God, the Sovereign Lord of this universe.

And that's what M. N. "Cotton" Robinson was. He was just who he was. I am always amazed at the prophet's insight. God has given me eyes to see through when I talk with Joe. Now I know, now I really do understand better, much better. I understand why he won those seven state championships and well over a hundred straight district games—he was a genius. No pretense, no façade, no arrogance about him, he was just Cotton Robinson.

I honestly believe many of us spend our entire lifetime trying to be something we're not. I wonder how many people out there today want to be a Tiger Woods or Michael Jordon or Lance Armstrong or Madonna? But life can be so much richer, so much more full, even complete when we are just being ourselves.

It is said of the great eagle that he flies so effortlessly by simply catching the updraft of the winds. Then he simply soars as he allows the winds to carry him. He doesn't work at it as we would imagine.

Through the eyes of the prophet I sense a renewed freedom after talking with him about this Texas Hall of Fame coach, Cotton Robinson. He reminded me of who I am, of my own limitations and potentials. He reminded me, too, that greatness is often God-given. He also said to my heart that you and I need to be the best we can at the position God has placed us in life. He is our life Coach. And we must dedicate ourselves to be the best we can be where we're at, while there's time until He calls us home.

"Everything about you is unique."

YOU

Now just think about all the people in this world, and you are unlike any other person. Your looks, your talents, your gifts, your abilities and ideas, your dreams and your hopes, your eyes and your nose, even your teeth and your hair are different from all the other billions on this green earth.

No wonder the Psalmist in the Bible asked, "What is man that You (God) are mindful of him?"

Do you realize your value? Who are you? Think about it. Why are you even on this planet?

Everything about you is unique. From your lips to your little toe, from your heel to your forehead, you are the apple of God's eye. He made you for Him; for Himself.

I often ask people, have you engendered an elbow lately in your lab? Of course, you haven't. A real elbow, too?

What potential you and I have! God has endowed us with so very much. You underestimate yourself, and so do I. Satan wants to make dirt out of your life; he's out to kill, steal and destroy everything about you. He likes nothing better than to see you with negative thoughts and pessimistic beliefs and ideas.

You. You. You. You are it. You can be anything you want to be. As someone once taught us in history, "You can't saw sawdust." The very entanglement which we allow to bring us down is the "past." Learn to let go. You are that important to God and to yourself and to others. Past failures, guilt, and old grudges will suffocate you and your effectiveness to live victoriously. Let it go.

Say to yourself, "It's Over!"

Why is God mindful of you? He made you. He made you for a purpose. He loves you. He is your heavenly Father. As one minister describes it, "Your picture is on His refrigerator." Or as I say, "He carries your picture in His wallet."

You. Who are you? To God you are more important than all the diamonds in this world, more important than all the planets which light up a star-filled night, more valuable than all the gold in Fort Knox, and more significant than all the skyscrapers which grace the cities over this earth.

Just think about it. There will never be another you - not in this lifetime or any other. Remind yourself of who you really are—you are a gift from God to mankind. He made you for a purpose. You are the only you that will ever exist. Your smile, your dimples, your chin, your cheeks, even your eyebrows are one of a kind. Do you know how much you're worth? Really? Do you?

David wrote in his psalm, "I praise you because I am fearfully and wonderfully made." My, how true! There ain't another like you, not a one. You. You. You.

"He (God) knows our possibilities."

YOU (Part Two)

I've seen them walking quite often through the neighborhood. Both are crippled and have permanent disabilities; anyone can tell this by careful observation. It actually appears like both of them are in great pain as they take every step to walk down the sidewalk. Often, when I am wrestling with all the stresses and difficulties of a day, when I see them I am suddenly renewed within just knowing how blessed I really am. Dear God their pain! It is so visible, and I--I am able to walk with so much less effort. "Why Lord?" I always ask when I see these two people giving every effort they've got just to make each step.

I am also reminded of who you and I are. You are something else! Why? Because God is something else! Your ability to draw or paint or write or play well in sports; your talent as a musician, your affinity to cook or sew; your ability to make money or soar through the computer software; you who can run a business; you who can mother a family; you who defends a defendant successfully in a court of law, you who can run a victorious campaign in politics; you who can soar through space as an astronaut...you are something else. Whether you're an actor or doctor, teacher or plumber, preacher or lawyer, speaker or promoter, sports star or race driver, adventurer or climber, common worker or professor, project manager or tanner, whoever you are you are something else in God's binoculars.

You have inside yourself unlimited resources which can be found by believing in yourself and in God. You have the potential to turn that health problem around, to start another business, to overcome the gnawing depression that haunts you, to overcome the incredible debt you owe. You, that's right, you are filled with potential beyond even your wildest dreams. You are endowed with possibilities that God has given you as a gift from His divine and almighty hand. You and I have not even touched the surface of our capabilities and powers. Inside our brain lie several billion cells that make up this awesome computer—what a reservoir to draw from every day!

The tragedy is that many of us never draw out that sweet, cool water from the well of our soul.

You really are like that old Gaither song, *"You are a promise, you are a possibility."* Just because you're not written up in the newspaper each month, or seen on TV, or don't hear your name over the radio or internet, somebody else does—God. That's right, God does. He sees us in the light and in the blackest of nights. He knows our possibilities. He gave gifts to you. Use them, for heaven's sake. Let that music out of you.

Our brain is the same brain that thinks positive, and it's the same brain that thinks negative. You and I employ so little power of our brain. Maybe it's because of fear, maybe it's because of past teachings, maybe it's because of the habits (the ruts) we've formed over many years and we've adopted them for security reasons. Whatever it is, you and I use a very small portion of our brain power. But that power, that potential, is there to be accessed, not buried.

After his death Einstein was cremated, but his brain soaked for decades in a jar of formaldehyde in the possession of Dr. Thomas Harvey, the Princeton Hospital pathologist. In the 1980s bits of Einstein's gray matter were studied by leading neurobiologists who learned nothing really, but that is was just a brain. Why? Because there was not a heart and soul and body working with it.

You are more than just a body part. You are more than just another chapter to a book. You are creation's highest and noblest being. You are somebody. Whether you think you are or not. Whether your boss thinks you are or not. Whether your parents or spouse or whoever may be taking you for granted this side of heaven, you are somebody.

Take a real good look at yourself in the mirror today and say to yourself, "I AM SOMEBODY." And you are, and you always will be. God made you and He will take care of you no matter what anyone else may say or think. You are a special you; never forget it. And there's only one of you in this whole wide world and there will never be another.

> "Your hands made me and formed me"........(Psalm 119:73).

"What a gift when we give ourselves to others."

THE GIFT

"Ronnie," she explained, "my dad stayed with his church even though I was freed from the concentration camp back during the World War II days. We were of Japanese descent, so we had to go to the prison camps right here in our own country—the U.S. We were Americans, too, Japanese Americans."

I said, "That is extraordinary, just extraordinary!"

It was the early forties, Pearl Harbor and all of that world confusion was going on that most people now don't even remember or know about. But those who lived through it, they remember, and remember well. They remember what a morose time it was in American history.

"Ronnie," she continued, "I was only a small child back then. They let me go about a year earlier even though I was Japanese. My memory is vague to this day why they released some and others were kept in the camps...my father was a Christian. He was a devoted Japanese Methodist minister, too. I remember he chose to stay with his church until they were all released. I got out with my mother and a relative for some reason."

For a moment my heart sank. I thought about just how people treat people in war times. How people forget the value of a human soul. How people, like Hitler, could ever sanction an Auschwitz. How boundaries are drawn by race and culture and religion and philosophy.

I am also reminded of those 183 men who committed their lives to General William B. Travis and the freedom of Texas. They, too, chose to stay in the camp. It was 1836. It was at the famed Alamo, an old mission which became a fort in San Antonio, Texas. General Travis took his sword out and drew a line in the sand. He said to those who would stay that they must step across the line if they wanted to fight for a free Texas. Many walked away that day, but 183 stayed. They all met their fate. But to this day we still hear those words, "Remember the Alamo!"

I probably will never know this devoted Methodist minister, but I will always remember this story just like I have remembered the Alamo where I've visited many times. My clients teach me more than I could ever learn at some big financial conference or investment convention. This faithful Methodist minister reminds me of the Old Testament prophet. Ezekiel. Remember, he went to be with the exiles at Tel Abib near the Kebar River. And God's Spirit led him to "sit among them for seven days."

What a gift when we give ourselves to others! Most children grow up today wanting so much to have a father and mother to spend time with them. We all know that this is the greatest gift we can give to a child—ourselves; definitely not another plastic toy that will go out with the garbage a month or two later.

When our oldest grandson comes over to see us his first question is, "Pa Pa can we play?" Davin is wanting me, not a toy or a thing or an object...just Pa Pa.

1995 was the worst year I spent on this planet. Nothing went right for me as an estate legacy planner. It seemed like every case I tried to open and close was straight up hill and then some. There really are no words for such an experience in life, for such unbelievable heart ache, but Nancy (my wife) and I went through it. She urged me to get out of the business I was in. It was a year that was wrapped up like a stormy day with darkness, dreariness, depression, and discouragement. I don't have enough words to describe it.

I remember coming home one day and there was nothing in our pantry. I actually took some hub caps that I had collected and went and sold them for $34 so we could have food on our table. That was the school of hard knocks and horrific blows.

My, how things can change in life! I went to an old minister friend and told him that I was at the end of my rope. He told me, "Ronnie, there's only one answer when things get so bad that we can't handle them anymore, and that's found on our knees. So we dropped to our knees and Jack asked God to turn my life and my business and my future around for me and for my family."

I remember that Christmas was the most memorable Christmas I've ever had. I didn't receive any gifts. I really didn't want any either. It was a very bleak Christmas, to say the least, if you had to add it up in tangible gifts. I remember it like yesterday, sitting there with my family before me—I honestly think that Christmas taught me what Christmas is really all about. I did receive some-thing I think which was greater than any gift I've ever gotten at Christmas - I received the gift- commitment.

I also recall telling my wife that I was going to make it in this business if it meant selling my own blood. It finally dawned upon me that my business required "staying, and sticking no matter what, it demanded total commitment." And I did just that, just like the Japanese Methodist minister. I could have easily walked out of the camp, but I made up my mind that I was staying no matter what.

There are no words now to express to God how wonderful and marvelous and unbelievably gracious He has been to me since then. God has overshadowed me and my business and my life and my family with innumerable blessings. He has turned my business into a ministry really. I would never share this to brag, but hope-fully to encourage you out there to never give up or in or out; with God anything is possible. He can turn dark, deep dungeon-like valleys into bright, high mountain peaks you never dreamed you could reach.

And as the Psalmist says so well, "Blessed be the Lord, who daily loads us with benefits" (Psalm 68:19 NKJV).

It's funny how God works sometimes. Nancy (my wife, or Nancy Jean as we call her sometimes) and I were eating out with friends not long after I had prayed with my old pastor friend, Jack. And a Mr. Glen Jeffrees, the late Mr. Glen Jeffrees, looked me right in the eyes and said emphatically, "Ronnie, you are going to be very successful one day in your business. I believe in you, I really do."

I kind of chuckled asking, "You really think that Glen?"

And he came right back, "I know you are! You are going to do well and you are going to be very successful at what you do."

And then Erline, his wonderful wife chimed in with him, "Ronnie, Glen believes in you. He's not just saying that. He really believes you are going to be successful at what you do."

Wow! Here I had just come off the worst year of my whole life and this is the message Glen gave me. Now his picture, which I drew with my own hand, hangs in our offices in Denver. I walk by him every day and he still reminds me, "Ronnie, you are going to be very successful at what you do. I believe in you, I really do."

I don't know who you are that's reading this today, but you and I share the greatest gift of all, a commitment that was given many years ago by a man who "treaded the winepress alone." His name was Jesus. He did not desert his church either. He gave His life in the camp, too. And I've got some good news for you. He believes in you, too.

"No one in this life ever arrives."

THE APPRENTICE

Aren't we all? You know, an apprentice in this life? I remember growing up in Southeast Texas and being around men who were plumbers and carpenters and electricians. My dad and his brother had a very successful heating and plumbing company. By nature of the contracts which they acquired, we would meet and work with other skilled workers out on a job; myself, just a high school kid trying to pick a little extra spending money.

Some of the workers were foremen, one or two a supervisor, and then you'd hear the words journeyman and apprentice. It seems like I worked around an apprentice the most. They were younger men and were trying to learn the ropes of the business. They were always having to study more and take tests, too. Now and then they'd go to a journeyman and get their problems solved.

As I look back on those days now I realize more and more that all of us are apprentices in life. We never get too old to learn and should always be studying. That's what I liked about the little book, *Tuesdays With Morrie*. In this story a dying professor is telling us to go on with life, to keep learning and inspiring others. You can just tell he wants other people to know the marvelous opportunities we have this side of the grave, and the value we should place upon our time and our relationships with family and friends.

The dictionary says an apprentice is, "a person learning a craft under a skilled worker."

When I think of an apprentice I think about Moses of old. He told the Lord that they would not believe him if he went back to Egypt, and that he was not eloquent in speech. He added, "I am slow of speech, and of a slow tongue." Moses was saying in essence, the Lord would have to find somebody else to lead the Children of

Israel out of Egypt.

Moses, in fact, made the Lord angry over his comments. Here was a true apprentice in every way when it came to being a spokesman for God. And yet look how God used an apprentice to lead millions to freedom.

If you feel like sometimes you are of no use to anybody and that you're just an apprentice in life, please think again. We are always learning more. No one in this life ever arrives. In fact, just when you think you have arrived, you'll find out just how ignorant you really are.

I remember years ago when I first preached, my late mother-in-law said that I asked the congregation at the end of the service to "bow their eyes and close their heads." And my older brother told me when I preached on Samson one night that I called him Samuel at least thirty-one times in my message. Probably the worst thing I ever said in a pulpit mistakenly, of course, was to a church who desperately needed to get organized. And I rifled off on a Sunday morning if you can believe this, "This church needs to have an orgasm if it's ever going to move forward."

An apprentice is going to get his/her nose bloodied. You're going to be like Blaine, our second oldest grandson, who trips every time he comes into our home because the last step is just a little too high for his stride. You're gonna trip a lot, make mistakes, wish to God you were dead and think that the world has come to an end for you, but never ever give up . Everybody's an apprentice in God's eyes, and we all need His grace and His divine mercy.

One of the most honest resumes you'll ever read is found in the Holy Scriptures. It's from a herdman of Tekoa. He was working with his animals in pastures and God called him to an assignment. If anybody was an apprentice, it was this man. But God used him in spite of his little expertise because he had an obedient heart.

He, was such a faithful prophet that he was asked to leave where he was preaching because "the land was not able to bear all his words" (including the king of that day, Jeroboam, king of Israel). But Amos's answer was, "I was no prophet, neither was I a prophet's son; but I was a herdman, and a gatherer of sycamore fruit: and the Lord took me as I followed the flock, and said unto me, Go, prophesy unto my people Israel " (Amos 7:14, 15).

If that's not an apprentice, nobody is. But look how God used this man! God wants to use us, too. Every smile we give to this world, every encouragement, every inspiration, every good witness for Christ and every helping hand, apprentice or not, God can magnify for His great glory and honor.

So don't you feel like you're just an apprentice in life. We all are. We all need one another. You have a gift and talent that God can do wonders with, He just needs your heart as well. As the great preacher Spurgeon once said, "God employs his people to encourage one another." People can call us a flop or failure all they want. God sees you as the biggest potential on His squad. In fact, I believe He's looking for apprentices just like you and me.

"... his parents gave him so much room full of hope and charcter and love."

NO ROOM FOR FAILURE

Nancy and I were having just another relaxing evening. We were watching Bill O'Riley's show and drinking our Swiss Mocha. After one or two guests, Mr. O'Riley had the great Mr. Barry Sanders, running back for the Detroit Lions.

"Now come on Barry, why did you leave $20 million on the table and just walk away? I don't understand it, sports fans don't, and many of the players and coaches and owners still haven't figured this one out."

Barry muttered a few answers and Bill came right back at him. O'Riley wasn't going to let Barry get away with a soft answer.

Then Barry raised an eyebrow when Bill continued to question him about all those **vices**, too. "Why is it, Barry, you just never got into that drug scene and booze and sex and all those things that become so available to the pro's like yourself?"

Barry responded with a confidence in his voice that heaven could hear, "Bill, you'd have to know my upbringing. How my parents taught me and laid the foundation for my life. I had **no room for failure** the way they brought me up."

Man, when I heard those words I said to myself, what parents! God forbid if they were not privy to hear such a marvelous compliment by their child. I don't know Mr. and Mrs. Sanders, but I would give anything to sit down with them, just meet them and talk with such incredibly unique people in a world of so much sexual promiscuity, child abuse, and moral rebellion.

No room for failure. Boy! What a world, what a nation this would be today if every child could say what Barry Sanders said on this

TV talk show. "I had **no room for failure**."

Today in America we know that in 1998 an estimated 3,154,000 children were reported to child service agencies as alleged victims of child abuse or neglect. Approximately one million of these were confirmed. Just imagine how many were never reported or even known.

Approximately three children died each day in the United States from abuse or neglect in 1997. Can you believe that? God help us. While some parents give their children **no room for failure**, others make their own children a complete failure and even kill them.

One-half of all Americans believe child abuse and neglect is the most important public health issue facing this country, compared to other public health issues like drug and alcohol abuse, heart disease, cancer and HIV/AIDS.

Goodness! From sex offenders to rapists, from child porn to criminal negligence, you'd think that Americans would get the picture, but we haven't, not really. Some months ago here in Colorado a lady jetted off to Europe leaving several of her small children behind to fend for themselves. She had fallen in love with a new boyfriend.

I certainly don't have the answer, but I do feel much like Billy Graham's daughter who was interviewed recently on national TV. She was asked about prayer in the schools today, how she felt about it. And she said in essence, "God has been a gentleman and stepped back and allowed us to omit prayer and Bibles and religious freedoms in our schools and now we are paying for it."

It's been just a few years ago when I was returning home from Parker, Colorado, that I heard a radio announcer come on the air and say, "Something really bad is happening at Columbine High School right now, and if you're religious I hope you will pray for the safety of all the students there and faculty."

At that point I did pray and everything was sketchy. Later, of course, shock waves were sent around this state and country and even throughout the whole world of what Eric Harris and Dylan Klebold had done.

When I think of what Barry Sanders said, "I had **no room for failure** because of my upbringing," and then to think that two kids went on a selfish rampage and snuffed out the lives of twelve innocent students and a faithful teacher, it is a marvel to me. Just think if Mr. and Mrs. Sanders, Barry's parents, had had the opportunity to give Eric Harris and Dylan Klebold just some of their principles while these two kids were growing up; what a difference it would have made. Lives would have been spared, too.

It was a Sunday afternoon that I visited the memorial sites of those fallen victims. I had spoken on the west side of Denver that day. I decided to go by Columbine and show my respect; it was the last day before they were to remove the memorial sites.

It had rained heavily the day before, and when I arrived people were in light coats and walking all around this campus. A very light misty-type rain still filled the air, but not enough to get you wet. Parking was almost impossible because of so many cars. There were thousands of people on hand. The media was still everywhere. Large trucks with satellite dishes became a backdrop to this awful and yet touching scene.

And you know, as I walked by each memorial step by step, I could hear my own squishy sound and that of others near me as we toured this tragic scene upon this rain soaked, makeshift memorial site. I have never, ever heard such deafening silence in the company of so many people in my entire life - especially outdoors like this. Even a hush fell upon the small children who walked beside their parents. Only a faint sound now and then filled the air from cars in a distance traveling slowly by the school.

As one student wrote and left a note that day near Cassie Bernall's memorial, "Even heaven is shedding tears today over the loss of such wonderful souls and innocent lives."

I was so moved by this scene that I took my pen out and just began recording poem after poem and article after article by family, friends and students who had written something to vent their terrible loss and devastating sorrow.

And now, as I look back upon this unnecessary murderous event in our country's history, in the Land of the Free and the Brave, I cannot help but hear the words of this great running back for the Detroit Lions, Barry Sanders, "I had no room for failure." Whatever his parents taught him, however, stuck! Because they taught him so well he's now teaching us. He had no room for failure because his parents gave him so much room full of hope and character and love.

The very first verse of scripture we taught our children was from the New English Bible Version: "Start a boy out on the right road and when he is old he will not depart from it" (Proverbs 22:6 NEB).

"As the twig is bent, so grows the tree," is an old quote. I hope you can experience what Barry Sanders and I have; my parents gave me no room for failure, too. What indebtedness I have to two people who taught me, gave to me, cared for me and loved me!

When you're given no room for failure, you can be sure you've been given a lot of room for success.

"... you just feel better as a person when you really work hard and accomplish a lot for others and yourself."

REACHING BACK AND GETTING IT!

My brother who docs construction in Southeast Texas said to me once, "You gotta reach back and get it!" Kenny was referring to a job I once helped him on.

Right before I had to put my long time best friend Pugsley (our Boston Terrier) down, I took him on a short walk. I recall that morning for the first time I can remember in years I didn't feel like going to my office to work. It wasn't the actual work I do that I dreaded, I was just beat physically; you know, kind of run down and didn't feel like reaching back and getting anything.

But on our walk that morning about 5:30 a.m. I looked up on the roof of the little elmentary school near our home. And as Pugs and I walked I saw at least twenty men working like Turks as they were re-roofing the school. Boy! They were "really reaching back and getting it." Believe me, these men inspired me to get to my office as quickly as possible. And I did.

How you define life determines your destiny. Your perspective will influence how you spend your time, spend your money, use your talents and value your relationships. ₁ I truly believe worry, not hard work, kills most people when all is said and done.

And you know, you just feel better as a person when you really work hard and accomplish a lot for others and yourself. So whoever you are who reads this, I hope in some way I have inspired you to "reach back and get it today."

1. Rick Warren, *The Purpose of Deam Life* (Grand Rapids, Michigan: Zondervan, 2002)

SALVATION AND REDEMPTION

"There is no exit from the cross or around the cross."

OUR INDEBTEDNESS IS TOO MUCH

I am talking to a young Asian pastor and we have just met, and I am enthralled by his presence and by his love for the Lord and the ministry he has been called into. Somehow in our conversation he and I begin talking about the Messiah and all that He gave to us through His death on the cross. Then in his eyes I notice how the young pastor looks upward toward heaven. He blurts out, "Ronnie, our indebtedness is too much to Him and for Him."

My, how that pierced my heart and my soul! I got to thinking just about what that man said. "Our indebtedness is too much to Him and for Him." Just how do you pay a debt to Someone who has not only given His life for you, but Who has done so innocently. He is one who covered the total payment of all your sins: your lying and cheating, cursing and sneaky ways, moral and willful mistakes have all been hidden behind Calvary's cross. How can you repay Someone like this who, in fact, is the Son of the living God and who is indeed God, Himself—your Creator and Savior and King and Lord? He is the same One who breathed the very breath of life into your nostrils.

We just think we have a big bill to pay down here when we buy a new house or car or diamond ring or business investment or credit card debt, but how do we pay Christ the Lord for all of His dying love and compassionate care which He showed us at Calvary? Remember, "Greater love has no man than this, that a man lay down his life for you" (St. John 15:13 KJV).

Just how much debt do we have toward Jesus Christ, the Son of the living God? Most people want to feel that if they follow their conscience and do the right thing to the best of their ability and serve others as much as possible and follow the Golden Rule and help the poor now and then and give to charities...they will go to heaven. Not so! Sorry, but God's system just doesn't work that way, never has and never will.

This is why the Lord declared when He was on this planet, "I am the way, the truth and the life, and no man comes to the Father but by me." There is no exit from the cross or around the cross. Although it was a beastly, gory, shameful and horrible and inconceivable death, it was God's way of paying for our sins and the awful curse debt which sin brings upon us all. And oddly enough, rather than grieve over Christ and His incredible and "unmatchable" sacrifice, we should only rejoice and praise our God in heaven because He did it willingly and perfectly and redemptively for you and me.

This is exactly why we celebrate Easter every year, which most people, sad to say, don't even know what it's about. But this is the day we celebrate when Christ came forth out of the tomb, came back to life. It is our victory day. It is the reminder that although our indebtedness is too much to Him, we know He came through for us and paid the ultimate price for our salvation through His own blood.

"But God was not late on His payment."

PAID IN FULL

We have all received a statement through scripture, "Paid in Full." The payment was made by our heavenly Father through the gift of His only Son, Jesus Christ. God in every way is a business person. He chose to make such an inestimable payment.

We all receive those statements and bills on the fifteenth and thirtieth of each month. We know how hard it is to make those payments, too. Often we can't, or at least not on time. We have all been there. No money! Out of work. Late payments. This is life and this is us, humanity.

But God was not late on His payment. He was on time. And He had sufficient funds. And the payment was the sacrifice of His Son, Jesus.

This payment was paid in full. There are no more payments to be made. It is over, finished, complete. There are no installment issues, no other statements to be sent out, no more records to be kept or spread sheets to be filled out. You are free of any debt.

God has underwritten the whole thing. Yes, it was expensive and painful, hard, and overwhelmingly huge. How do you value your only son or daughter or spouse? In this case it was His own Son. How do you give up a child? Just think. We worry about our children even when they leave the house, much less to give them up in a cruel, merciless death. But that was the payment.

Everything we do down here evolves around paying. It doesn't matter what it is; there is going to be a payment made in order to transact business and living expenses. Whether it is eating, sleeping, entertainments, business, travel, clothing, taxes, or dying we are faced with payments. So it is with salvation.

Christ is a must. No Christ, no payment for our sins. His job was a payment with His life, and that's what He did. He gave His life so that we might have our sins taken care of. Our salvation came out of God's wallet. Without Christ, we were without hope. Following Moses and the Commandments just weren't enough. Following all the laws in the world were not enough; there still had to be that one thing—the payment for sin. Christ did exactly that.

This is why there are some places you just can't get in. No payment, no entrance! It is only after the payment that you can acquire an entrance. Otherwise the door is shut. The security guards will oust you. Whether it is a movie, a play, or a ballet, we must pay. Whether is a game, a trip, or a meal, we must pay. There are no free lunches in life. No payment, no enjoyment! No payment, no entertainment!

Do any of us have any earthly idea of just how much salvation's payment was? We hear preachers and teachers and professors and educators attempt to explain this payment, but how can anyone? How do you ever explain or understand the Creator of this universe, giving up His own Son in such a horrible sacrificial death on a cross? It really is far-reaching. What an incredible payment. How costly! Mindboggling, and yet God did it.

"...we are ready for that 'abundant entrance'."

THE ABUNDANT ENTRANCE

We often take for granted doors we enter until we come upon those most unusual ones. I remember visiting NORAD in Colorado Springs, Colorado, some years ago along with my wife and a group from our church. One of our members was on good terms with a soldier who could get us inside this incredible facility built inside Cheyenne Mountain.

NORAD stands for the North American Air Defense Command. This giant hole in a mountain is entered through the widest and probably the most secure doors in the world. They appeared to be at least three feet thick. I would not try to estimate the other dimensions of these doors. Inside, of course, is a small town made of everything you can imagine, from buildings to a small lake, to every kind of conceivable amenity one would need in the event of a nuclear war. I remember going through those doors just like it was yesterday; what security I felt!

Think back of all those doors and entrances you've made in life. Just imagine every day being the President of this great nation and passing through the White House doors to do business for millions of people in this country and people throughout the world. I don't know about you, but I've been privileged to enter a lot of incredible places in my lifetime. From a governor's office to Elvis's Graceland Mansion, from a 747 airplane to a big cruise liner, from the door where Jesus was believed to have been buried and rose again, to the old home place of my roots in what we call Deep East Texas, namely Center, Texas.

Entrances are made by us every day. We go through garage doors and the boss's door sometimes; we go through big entrances and small ones. In Mexico I remember going through the door of a hut to visit an elderly blind woman. She had memorized the entire Bible over her lifetime. Her hut was one room with a fireplace-like stove right in the middle of the little abode. Her hair was white, her skin tanned and very wrinkled, and her countenance was glowing with the love and grace of God.

Through our translator she told me that her village (Lahoya, about 10,000 feet upon a mountain) was established as a Christian village, but rebels were starting to come in and cause problems. One could just tell that little lady had nothing of this world's riches or stuff, but I've never forgotten making that entrance into her small hut.

When I served on a board in Southeast Texas for Lamar University we would have meals catered to us when we would meet at the university's branch in Orange, Texas, which was held at the Brown Center. What a palatial landmark it is in such a small community! Edgar Brown was a very wealthy Texan who left his mansion to charity—and Lamar University took over the property.

One of the custodians who knew all about this incredible mansion took me on a private tour through this marvelous edifice. As we made our way through one of the final doors, he said this was Mr. Brown's secret getaway passage. It was a narrow escape passage which led to an outside door in the event that robbers might come in to steal and to kill. Wow! How do you ever forget an entrance and an exit like this one? You don't!

Entrances. We go through them every day of our lives. Elevators, automobiles, airplanes, trains, buses, buildings, homes, offices, bank vaults, malls, shops, and hotels we enter and seldom think about the final entrance. What about that entrance? One day St. Peter will be waiting for us, won't he?

I have a little book at home that I often read authored by the great preacher Charles Spurgeon. I find myself always going back to this one little devotional paragraph. He writes:

You see yonder ship. After a long voyage, it has neared
the haven, but is much injured; the sails are rent to ribbons. That is like the righteous being "scarcely saved."
But do you see that other ship? It has made a prosperous
voyage; and now, laden to the water's edge, with the sails
all up and with the white canvas filled with the wind; it
rides into the harbor joyously and nobly. That is an "abundant entrance;" and if you and I are helped by God's spirit
to add to our faith, virtue, and so on, we shall have at the
last an "abundant entrance into the kingdom of our Lord
Jesus Christ."[1]

Entrances. Our bodies and our minds make them everyday. With
our minds we enter a new world of knowledge and challenges and
stuff we have to cope with constantly in our busy schedules. Just
like our bodies entering places, we make choices with our minds
to enter places day after day. These entrances affect us and everyone around us; what we choose means whether we will win or
lose. As my friend the prophet has said, "Ron, we're all given a
deck of cards, and how we play them will mean our end whether it
is for good or for bad."

It has been years since I walked inside the Great Pyramid of Egypt.
I remember that entrance so clearly, even today. The temperature
was 72 degrees, too. It was just like it was built for, too, a tomb.
Utter silence gripped my heart. As I stood there I could just imagine an ancient king entering for the first time after its completion
along with his entourage. What an entrance that must have been!

In the conference room of my company is a painting of the Eastern
Gates to Jerusalem. It is an original from an artist I paid to draw
from a picture I took when I was there in 1980. Muslims have built
a cemetery in front of those gates as a mockery toward Christianity
and the fictitious second coming of Christ—at least in their opin-
ion. But one day that final entrance will occur. As my dear friend
the old prophet once said:

"Ronnie one day that sun is going set again for the last

1. Charles H. Spurgeon, Daily Help (New York Gosset & Dunlap, 1978.)

time. Then it will come up shining just like it always has; nothing will have changed. But on this day something is going to be vastly different on the calendar of time. People will just be going about their usual schedules and errands to run. But it won't be that way with the Almighty. There will not be another day for work nor play, for paying bills or making money, for headaches or heartaches. This day His Son will gloriously return with the cloud of angels and every knee shall bow and every tongue shall confess that He is Lord. There won't be any question Who this Man is! How ironic! That day for all to see whether now, or a thousand years from now will be just another work day or weekend day, yet not with the Lord. And remember, only the Father knows when His Son will make that entrance; but just be sure of this, it will happen."

Thank God for those of us who are truly His and know Him through our personal faith, because of His marvelous grace we are ready for that "abundant entrance."

Whether our sails are rent to ribbons, or snow white and filled with the latest gust of wind, we anxiously await our "abundant entrance." Are you ready?

"There is no other rose like this in the valley of life."

THE ROSE OF SHARON

Just now and then do we catch the real drama of how it all came to pass. No novelist or author could ever drum up such a story, and no book has sold so many copies over the centuries.

It is Isaiah the prophet who seems to allude the most to the coming **Rose of Sharon**. But really, all through the Old Testament there is that Messianic hint and prophetic utterance that He is coming. Hundreds of years, centuries before He comes, it is written that He will indeed invade human history. And He did.

But there is that one thought which King Solomon, at least according to our reading, gives us about His coming which I think is one of the best and most descriptive to think about. He writes those touching and magical and most colorful words, "I am the **Rose of Sharon**" (The Song of Solomon 2:1).

What better portrait of the One we all long for and ultimately will bow our knees to and confess that He is the Lord, the Christ indeed. I am the **Rose of Sharon**. He was "a tender plant, a root out of dry ground" (Isaiah 53:2). Every petal about Him was pristine and perfect. Men ran to Him with their afflicted. Even children sought to sit upon His lap.

A rose? Yes, a rose! But not just any flower which had bloomed. This man was more than mere mortal. As the soldiers who were supposed to have apprehended Him declared, "We never heard a man speak like this before." No! And neither they, nor any of us ever will again. He was a supernatural savior.

He was the **Rose of Sharon**. In the midst of weeds and bushes and briars and thorns came this Galilean. To this day the world still does not know how to receive this Rose. Do I display it and honor it and adore it; or is this just another fake in this world? Who really is this **Rose of Sharon**?

Can I trust this religious stuff? And what makes Him so great, what makes Him the real thing? Why do I have to deal with Him?

Just keep sniffing, just keep listening, and you'll get there. Why? Because He is much more wanting to come to you than you are to Him. Remember He is the **Rose of Sharon**. There is no other rose like this in the valley of life. Just smell with your spirit and soul and you can sense His eternal presence and power.

Remember, when He spoke the storms minded. When He prayed it was like He perspired with drops of blood. When He called to the dead, they woke up. When He strutted across a sea, it became as hard as an oak wood floor. And when He applied His authority, even demons hid from His rosy odor.

What is a Rose? This Rose is certainly not just another flower. No, He is much more than that. He is beautiful. He is lovely. He demands our attention. He colors life. He inspires ah's! He has a depth about Himself that is insatiable. He exudes life. He cannot be copied or fabricated. A real rose reminds us of how life is to be lived and how life is to fade away. Coupled together, roses make a scented bouquet with a priceless fragrance and aroma. A rose is known for its soft, delicate petals of beauty. There is no replacement for a rose.

When I asked my wife, "Honey, what do you think of when you see a rose?"

She replied pensively, "The petals."

That's it, too. His petals of mercy and grace, of love and forgiveness, of goodness and kindness, of character and righteousness have reached this globe many, many times over. Spiraling steeples, stained glass windows, church bells and crosses of every kind grace the stage of this green earth. His petals bring hope to the hopeless and strength to the weak and faint-hearted. He is "the **Rose of Sharon**, the **Lily of the valleys**."

Nothing or no one has ever changed history more or brought mankind more good news than this **Rose of Sharon**. Right on the heels of the Dark Ages when mankind had fallen into more despair than ever before, came the **Rose of Sharon** bringing His perfume of life and light. And to this day the songs that have been sung, the books that have been written, the lives that have been changed, the churches that have been built, the poems that have been penned, the messages that have been preached, and the thousands of groups that have been formed all in His name have come from this **Rose of Sharon** and His everlasting aroma.

It is no wonder that day the centurion who beheld the death of this Rose declared excitedly and with confidence, "Surely this man was the Son of God!" Thank God His fragrance still lives on in the heart of every believer who knows Him and walks in His Spirit.

This summer in Denver I passed by what had to be the loveliest rose I ever saw as I went to see an elderly client of mine. She told me that a gardner in the complex where she lives attended to the garden where I saw the beautiful rose. What splendor! It was absolutely magnificent!   It is no wonder King Solomon wrote of the coming Christ as the **Rose of Sharon**.

Remember after His victorious resurrection how those women were challenged by the angel to go and tell the disciples that the **Rose of Sharon** was not in His grave, that He arose from the dead just like He promised? Do you recall that He met them on the way? Then "Good Morning!" he said. They fell to their knees, embraced his feet, and worshipped him (St. Matthew 28:96 TMV).

Their Rose was alive...again! I think when they held Him by His feet there was utter awe and such strong, gripping silence they could only hear their beating hearts. And in this awe and silence they worshipped the **Rose of Sharon** for the first time in their whole lives with every bit of strength and love and passion they could possibly muster.

I am the Rose of Sharon and the Lily of the valley. What a Rose He's been to you and to me! One day we can all sit at His feet and worship Him, really worship Him as we look upon His face forever and forever. What fragrance He's brought to all of us! What life! What hope! What peace of mind! What truth! And what love! What new meaning to out lives! What endearing friends he has brought into our lives, too. He is the **Rose of Sharon.** He is your greatest gift in this whole wide world. To miss Him is to miss life's most cherished and prized fragrance. Without Him you and I are nothing.

"... the most important thing of all is what we have in our hearts."

A VERY RARE EXPENSE

Jewelry, clothes, cars, houses, stocks, bonds, bank accounts, land and businesses, they all add up to everything when placed in the right perspective. Christ taught when he was upon this earth, "What should it profit a man if he gained the whole world and lost his own soul ?" (St. Matthew 16:26 KJV). I think you have to look very closely at that question to really appreciate what the Lord was saying.

Now think about that question for a moment. It does not say you can't gain the whole world and lose your own soul. The emphasis on this question is very subtle. Why? Because the real question here is where is your soul? Is it so wrapped up in this world that you have forgotten God? Is seeking success, making money, and living for yourself and your business so important that nothing or no one else matters? If this is the case you have lost your soul in this life already.

By the way, this can happen, too. You don't have to lose your soul in eternity only. You can lose your soul here as well. This happens when you lose the purpose and meaning for your existence. Where did you come from? Why are you really here anyway? And where are you going when you die? You are going to die, or did you count on this happening to you?

Things do matter down here. Money can't buy everything, but it makes life a lot more fun and comfortable and desirable. We can feed people with money. We can build churches and homes and hospitals and schools.

A person is kidding himself or herself if they do not want to be successful. No wonder the Jabez Prayer took this country in a rage. People want to be blessed a whole lot and they want their professions and businesses to be enlarged. They want God's hand upon them, and they want his continued guidance and power in their lives. Guess what? I do, too. This is normal. This is what God expects from us.

Now think with me a moment. Think about how successful somebody is who can fling stars into space, build a moon and a sun and a green earth for his own creatures to live upon. Don't you wonder what endlessness is? There is no end to this Sovereign. There is no end to His universes and creative powers. He is truly El (Lord), "Elohim." He is incomprehensible.

"In the beginning 'Elohim' (God, in Hebrew) created the heaven and the earth" (Genesis 1:1). If this is not success, nothing is.

But his greatest success came when he gave, not created. This was a very rare, salient expense. He gave his only begotten son to die for my sins and your sins. His plan was so successful that now temples and churches and missions and cathedrals and steeples and crosses are spread across this globe: from Africa to India, from Russia to China, from the USA to New Zealand, from Europe to the moon, Jesus lives on. What a rare expense!

Yes, things do matter here, and the most important thing of all is what we have in our hearts. Without Christ ".... we are of all men most miserable" (1 Corinthian 15:19), as the Apostle Paul put it. He makes everything something. Without Him life is lifeless and meaningless and hopeless. There really is no more rare expense than Christ the Lord. He is "the way, the truth and the life and no man comes to the Father except by me" (St. John 14:6).

No wonder in scripture we read, "He is the lily of the valleys. He is the fairest of ten thousand and the bright and morning star." He is an eminent friend, a rare expense indeed. His love helps you more than any other love that is offered - He helps you to know that you are loved, too. A very, rare expense!

"... God loves us in spite of what we've done or haven't done."

GRACE

Only a few people on this earth in comparison to the millions and even billions have experienced the love and grace that they are looking for. Most people have no clue about how much they have been loved and still are loved in spite of all the crazy things they've done wrong.

I am convinced that most people are longing for this grace, too. They are searching for such mercy and love in every direction but the right direction. They fill their week with work, making money, going to movies, eating out, watching the TV, shopping, hunting, attending sporting events, golfing, bowling, sewing, cooking, fulfilling their hobbies and even going to church, but they never have truly experienced the grace they are desperately searching for.

People are born into this world; they live their lives, have children, and die, yet never know just what marvelous grace is available to them. What a tragedy! There could be no greater gift to mankind, no greater expression of compassion and forgiveness, and incredible offer of longsuffering than this grace. It is sheer grace, too, because it never even had to be offered to you and me. It was provided to us because of grace. So we are recipients if we choose to receive this grace. It is grace from grace. It is God's grace, God's unmerited favor; what astounding love!

The dictionary could not say it any more plainly. The Merriam-Webster defines grace as, "unmerited help given to people by God (as in overcoming temptation)." You and I don't earn it, we can't make it and have no way to offer it—it's from heaven. You sure can't buy grace on a Wal-Mart shelf!

In the scriptures it says it best, "For God sent not His Son into the world to condemn the world, but that the world through Him might be saved" (St. John 3:17 KJV). Unlike most human beings think, God really does love us just as we are. We need not put on any airs, try to be any better than we are, try to improve our conduct, act more saintly, or achieve some incredible feat in this world— God loves us in spite of what we've done or haven't done. He loves us through and through, up one side and down the other. He loves us in spite of all our failures, faults, victories or defeats in this life.

Because of His love for us and to us, He provided enough grace for all of us by the gift of His Son on the cross to change us for eternity. God has made it possible to allow us to come to an understanding of why we're here, where we came from, and where we're going after life is over. When all is said and done, this life is brief upon this earth, and you only have one life to live down here.

Jesus himself taught, "Greater love has no one than this, than to lay down one's life for his friends" (John 15:13).

But the Lord also explained that we connect to God's grace when we accept Him as Savior from above. Christ taught, "For the Father himself loves you, because you have loved Me (Christ), and have believed that I came forth from God" (John 16:27).

When I look back now over almost sixty years of living in this life I am reminded of the grace my family and I have been shown by a dear friend that we lost recently. For over thirty years now she has always remembered us at Christmas time with special gifts. Even on our birthdays and other special occasions, she has sent us presents and money and things which we never did one thing for, and I feel that we really did not deserve. But she kept it up until her death only a few days ago.

Why anyone would love me so and my family so and give to us like she did is still beyond me. She really never had a lot in this life, but she sure gave a lot. In fact, right up to her own dying days she nursed the elderly, waiting on them hand and foot until their deaths. What an expression of grace! Real, authentic grace and compassion! Wow! Could she be one of those Jesus mentioned when He declared, "The first shall be last and the last shall be first in heaven?" (St. Luke 15:30). I think so.

What beautiful words from a man who knew an incredible amount about grace, the Apostle Paul wrote, "But where sin abounded, grace abounded much more" (Romans 5:20b).

When I think about all the things I have done wrong, and that this world has done wrong and people throughout history have done wrong, it is unimaginable to think that there would ever be enough grace to cover all of our sins. But there is plenty of grace for the sins that were made by the price that was paid. All the lying, cheating, stealing, lustfulness, rape, murder, greed, terrorism, hate, discrimination, self-righteousness, drunkenness , drug abuse, injustices, gossip and just sheer blunders that people have been guilty of have been covered by the cross of Christ. That's the good news.

"But God demonstrates His own love (grace) toward us, in that while we were still sinners, Christ died for us" (Romans 5:8).

Yes, it is <u>unmerited help</u>. Can't buy it. Can't conjure it up. Can't negotiate for it. Can't create it or manufacture it. Can't earn it. Can't bargain for it. Can't ever really understand it or really experience it until you accept it from God. And it's available today for everyone who wants it. No matter how much you've messed up, His grace can clean it up. Amazing! Yes! Amazing Grace!

"You will always be neck deep in dark, disturbing, drowning water when you try to live life by your own efforts and strength."

NECK DEEP

Do you ever feel neck deep in things? You know like paying bills, IRS problems, divorce issues, past failures, heart aches and headaches with a staff member or business associate, or just with the struggles of life like health issues and aging? Absolutely nothing could be more germane to being neck deep than the story of the prodigal son in the scriptures.

Probably no text has ever been written about more or preached from or studied than this little passage in the Gospel of St. Luke. The story is about two brothers. The younger asks for his inheritance and leaves home only to squander everything he has in a foreign country. The elder brother stays home, faithful to his father as always.

This younger kid winds up in a pigpen eating with the farm animals and finally comes to his senses. He realizes that he is about as neck deep in troubles as one can get. So he concludes that even his dad's servants at home are better off than he is. So he decides to go back home and just tell his father that "he's no longer worthy to be his son, just let me be one of your hired servants" (St. Luke 15:19).

The Psalmist in his Old Testament writings alludes to our subject by crying out to God in his dilemma, "Save me, O God! For the waters have come up to my neck" (Psalm 69:1 NKJV).

If anybody on this planet ever knew about coming close to drowning in neck-deep waters it was King David. From the threats and attempts on his life by King Saul and his own countrymen and family members, David knew what it was to be totally exhausted and fatigued in the swift, neck-deep currents of dark and deadly waters.

It happens! Those neck-deep waters just swarm around us over-night sometimes. Maybe a health issue, a very bad disappoint-ment, a tooth ache, a car wreck, an accident or failure on our part—suddenly we find ourselves drowning and spent with soaring wa-ters all around us. Just when we thought everything was going great, we've got too much on our plate.

Dr. Charles Swindoll refers to neck-deep as inner turmoil, and it reveals itself usually at some specific spot in our physical body. For some it is a sharp pain in the stomach, for others it's revealed in a headache or backache or leg cramp.

"Any number of things," he writes, "can trigger this feeling." They are common to all of us:

- Bad news
- Strong fears
- Strained relations
- Car accidents
- Almost running out of gas
- Dental work
- Late-night phone calls
- Earthquakes/Storms.[1]

In the case of this young prodigal son he became so neck-deep in waters that he was not only feeding those pigs, but eating with them as well. What a picture of all of us. Satan loves to kill and to steal and to make our lives a total wreck! He wants you over-weight, sick, depressed, hurt. and unconfident—nothing will make the Devil happier, absolutely nothing!

You know, it is so interesting to me, too, in this account that our Lord gave us that no one gave to this young man, no one cared for his soul. Can you imagine that? But in total contrast, when he went back to his father and to home, the dad ordered that the best robe be placed on his back after a big, warm, loving hug. He placed a ring on his hand, sandals on his feet, and began festivities be-cause of his safe return.

1 Charles Swindell, Living Beyong the Daily Grind (New York: Inspirational Press, 1988).

How funny and how strange! Here he was in a foreign country neck-deep in waters and about to drown. By going home to his father he was on a mountain top safe and sound. What incredibly opposite positions in this life! The foreigners gave him nothing, and yet his father gave him everything.

And trust me, the same can happen for you and me when we let the Father take the controls of our lives. You will always be neck-deep in dark, disturbing, drowning waters when you try to live life by your own efforts and strength. This is why God tells us, "Be still (reassured and confident; trusting) and know that I am God" (Psalm 46:10). Know that I (God) can take care of you in any storm or flood which you may face in your life.

My late mother-in-law, Nanny, always prayed the most touching prayer when she offered grace or prayed out loud in public. And she always started with those same, familiar words, "Our kind and most gracious heavenly Father...." When you think about it, He really is a kind and most gracious heavenly Father who "loads us daily with many blessings and benefits" (Psalm 68:19). I don't know about you, but I've been neck-deep more than once in those deep, dark troubling waters of life. If I may be personal, I've been through nine major and minor surgeries, in a total of seven car wrecks, two head-on car wrecks; had our car hit by a large boulder in the Rocky Mountains after a storm, in a coma and blind for three days and nights from an allergic reaction, gone through several hurricanes, and had lighting dance at my feet with claps of thunder almost bursting my ear drums. So I know what it means to be neck- deep in water.

But whoever you are reading my words this day, just remember there's a loving, kind and most gracious heavenly Father just waiting to receive you. He has more love and mercy and grace than you can imagine, no matter what you've done or what you've been through, or what you're going through. He loves you like no other person can or will under the sun. And when you run back to Him he'll surprise you with gifts of compassion you can't believe. He'll rescue you from those deep, dark troubling waters you've been in far too long.

"Let them know there is sill hope."

REDEMPTION

It's been years now since I was in Miami at the Super Bowl in 1979. Nancy's brother and I saw Roger Staubach and Terry Bradshaw go head to head. Dallas had trailed, as I remember, 35 to 14 going into the second half of play. The Steelers turned the ball over toward the end of the game and Dallas almost came back and won the game. But they were inside the 5 yard line when the game clock ended. The final was 35 to 31 in favor of Pittsburg.

These were the years of Tom Landry and the emerging of America's Team. I recall getting there early with Barry and watching the Cowboys arrive in their chartered buses. We were able back then to pat the Cowboys on their backs as they entered the stadium from their chartered buses. It was the first time I remember that there had been threats of terrorism, too. So all kinds of mounted policemen and even the National Guard units were scurrying and scampering around the Orange Bowl stadium with their heavy weaponry.

Bradshaw had a terrific game and received the MVP award. He threw four touchdowns. And at the end of the game he literally raced across the field and hugged Roger's neck. I will always believe that he had that much respect for Staubach. Deep down inside he knew that game could have gone either way.

How strange it is that after all these years I ran into Roger Staubach at an airport sometime ago. We talked about that Super Bowl and Bradshaw and how they almost came back and won the game. We talked about Jackie Smith missing that pass which Roger threw right into his stomach in the end zone. It just wasn't meant to be; and I give the Steelers credit, they were the greatest that year.

The most important thing of all that I saw at the '79 Super Bowl, however, had nothing to do with the Super Bowl game between the Cowboys and the Steelers. It had to do with what I call redemption.

Only days before the Super Bowl a legendary coach named Woody Hayes had made the mistake of a lifetime. A young man named Charlie Bauman intercepted a pass from Ohio State in the last minute of play in a 17 to 15 win by Clemson in the Gator Bowl. As Bauman went out of bounds on the Ohio State sideline, Hayes lost total control and smacked the young man with his fists. Definitely inexcusable! It stunned sports fans all over the country.

Somehow Ohio State University forgot Woody's incredible 205-61-10 won-lost-tie record. It went out the door just like Woody Hayes did. Anyone in this nation who knew anything about sports didn't want to be near Woody Hayes. His very name brought an instant scowl to faces everywhere. He had become an overnight embarrassment to his university. To this day I don't think anyone who saw him smack that kid on the sideline can ever forget that December 31st Friday night incident.

We all waited to see the Dallas Cowboy football stars and cheerleaders and the coaches exit from the chartered buses which had arrived. One by one they started getting off the buses. Unbelievable excitement and enthusiasm filled the air. Fans were cheering, cameras were rolling and the press was on hand for the biggest sporting event of the year. Noise and clamor and ringing sounds and whistles brought magic to this august scene. People were everywhere. The anticipation was building higher and higher.

And then...at the end a man we all recognized with his little dude hat on (a man we knew as Tom Landry,) stepped off the bus with his arm around Woody Hayes. Coach Hayes had traveled to the stadium by invitation with the Cowboy's team. A hush came upon the crowd as though time itself stopped and no one really knew what to do or what to say or how to react. One or two started to boo! But somehow that didn't even last long because Tom Landry had his arm around the worst person you could think of at that time. You just wanted to hate this man for what he had done. You definitely didn't want to have any association with a coach who would slug an innocent young football player. What's goin' on here?

Now after all these years and the passing of Coach Landry, I realize more than ever what real coaching is all about. What real redemption is all about! What real caring and loving is all about! Coach Landry may have lost the Super Bowl that Sunday afternoon in Miami, but he saved a life, and gained the attention of the world—we shouldn't ever give up on human beings. When a person is down and has done it all wrong, that's when they need redemption the most. It's easy to help people along a smooth, clean life path, but it's not the same when you have to get down in a muddy, stinking, dingy, ditch to help them out.

There was a Coach many, many years ago who urged his team to go into all the world and redeem humanity with his gospel story. But in the end, they all forsook him. One even betrayed Him, another cursed him and denied that he even knew him. But he still put his arm around them in the end, and from a cruel cross he gave his own life for their sakes and for ours.

He, in fact, still places His arm around all those who will allow Him to. He has graciously promised us, "I will never leave you nor forsake you" (Hebrews 13:5b). Wow! What a Coach! What a caring, redeeming Coach!

Isn't there someone you and I know who needs that embrace of redemption? You know, someone who's blown it? Someone who has done it all wrong? Someone who is down on herself or himself? Someone who has given up on life? I urge you, as I do myself, to place your arm around some troubled soul today who has fumbled the ball in life. Let them know there's still hope.

The scriptures teach us that even "though a person's face is in the dust, there still might be hope (redemption)" (Lamentations 3:29).

The Lord reminds us, "In as much as you have done unto the least of these, you have done it unto me" (St. Matthew 25:40).

Someone out there is waiting for our arms of redemption every day.

ENCOURAGEMENT

"Release is what Exodus is all about."

RELEASED

Sometime ago, I became saturated with the Eleventh chapter of Hebrews, commonly known as the Hall of Faith in the Bible. As I scanned through the last chapters of this letter, which no one knows for sure who wrote, I stumbled upon that incredible thought at the end: "I want you to know that our brother Timothy has been released" (Hebrew 13:23).

Goodness, I got to thinking about what a wonderful and marvelous experience that must have been for Timothy and many other early Christians who finally secured their release so they could get back on the trail for Christ again and preach the good news.

Much of life becomes imprisonment for people because they either choose to live in such circumstances or they never discover the answer for their release. It doesn't matter whether it is from fears, anxiety, depression, insecurity, guilt, or those horrible, gnawing addictions which can ultimately steal and kill in the end.

I know a young man who became blind and went into a coma for several days from an injection he received which produced an allergic reaction. He said that in that room he saw and felt things that were so strange and disillusioning that his mind still goes back to that room of physical and psychological imprisonment.

I don't know if you've ever done a study on this word, release, but it's derived from an old Latin word where we get the root term for **(re)lax.** Makes sense doesn't it? If you're released from some duty or stressful experience in all likelihood you are going to be relaxed.

Ever been in the hospital for some extended period of time? Ever had your arm or leg in a cast for several weeks? Ever had some kind of dental brace for an extended period of time? Boy! What a release when it's over!

Ever paid forever on a revolving charge to make that purchase of something you just had to have? Ever paid for years on a loan for a piece of property and you finally got down to that last and final payment, then you cleared the books with that last check? What a release!

Release is what Exodus is all about. Moses and his millions of Hebrew children came out of Egypt. Nelson Mandela, who was imprisoned for years in South Africa, was finally released and now even rules as a leader. What release!

I saw a man interviewed some months ago who had been in prison for over twenty years for a crime he never did. Finally, through DNA testing, he was released from prison.

Over the years as a minister, families have asked me to go and see their family members who were incarcerated. I've been in city, county, state and federal jails and prisons. I guess I've seen it all, really. I've visited death row inmates and people serving time for far less severe crimes. I have always been amazed how strong, handsome, young, and talented children of God just like you and I could make such horrible and even stupid mistakes. "But for the grace of God there go I," as someone has appropriately said.

Release! Doesn't it just sound good? "I want you to know that our brother Timothy has been **released**." By the way, that's past tense. He was out, free, released, at liberty, at least for the present time.

In 1957 some Buddhist monks were going to move a clay Buddhist statue from a monastery in Thailand. They had to make way for a brand new highway. As the crane started to lift the large statue they noticed it began to crack. About this same time it started to rain as well, so they put the project on hold, and covered it with a canvas tarp.

Later that night the head monk went out to check on the Buddha. As he shined his flashlight on the statue he noticed something glimmering and shining back at him underneath the clay. So he quickly fetched a hammer and chisel and began chipping away at the Buddha. To his amazement he discovered that the whole ten-and-a-half-foot-tall Buddha was made of solid gold.

Now historians believe that centuries earlier Siamese monks, when Thailand was once called Siam, had undoubtedly covered this marvelous piece of craftsmanship with clay to protect their sacred god from destruction by the invading Burmese army. Today this Buddha is valued by some into the hundreds of millions of dollars.

But what a picture of humanity at its best! Much of our lives are lived in clay, imprisoned by so much baggage which we allow to control us and thwart our freedom. I'm convinced that much of this baggage is transferred down from earlier generations by which we have been taught. When you read the scriptures there are so many powerful formulas and techniques to overcome such baggage, too. These are solutions which can help set us free, but often we do not rely upon them. Christ taught us, "But you shall receive **power**..." and, "If the Son of man sets you free, you shall be **free indeed**" (St. John 8:36).

There is a golden risen, living Christ available to all of us if we want Him. And he is saying to you and me "I want you to know that our brother _________________ (write in your own name) has been released." Thank God our Christ is alive and does not come in a handmade statue. When and if you let Him get a hold of you, of your own life, you will be changed forever; all you have to do is **ask** Him. Then you can experience the "**release**" of a lifetime—you'll never, ever be the same again.

"The whole world is waiting to be loved."

POWER OF LOVE

With our ability to love, to really love others, ourselves and God we can change this world. Just as God gave His only Son to die for us, that same kind of love, that same kind of compassion, though not perfect like that of God's, can revolutionize societies.

Love is glorious. It truly is God. Think of the worst, most horrible wretched people who have ever lived and remind yourself that God loved them just as much as He loved us (and loves us). From Judas to Hitler, from Charles Manson to Osama bin Ladin - God has loved us all—definitely not because of what we do. Yes God loves us all in spite of what we do.

If you feel kind of left out or lonely, if you feel disappointed and dejected, your whole world and life can change by the power of love. Love transforms. Love is dynamite. Through the power of love you can do wonders for others and for yourself as well as for the Lord. The whole world is waiting to be loved.

When all is said and done, everyone just wants to be loved. Even the very meanest of people deep down inside are crying out for affection. Many people wrap themselves up so deeply and so intensely with their work and business, seeking only to be loved.

Love is the cry and heartbeat of every human being on this green planet. To be loved is to feel needed, and to feel needed is a reason for living, for real fulfillment down here. When love is absent, a morose spirit seems to invade human hearts. No love, no laughter. No love, no light…no hope.

Your beating heart and mine is beating for a purpose. We have been made for eternity, but we have been made for one another, too. Although we do get on each other's nerves, and greatly disappoint each other at times, we still desperately need each other and our love as well.

The baby needs the love of a mother and father. The newlywed craves the love of the new bride or groom. The aspiring son wants the love of his father. The student cries out for the nurture and love of the teacher. Love is very powerful. Strong. Magical. It is a part of life's recipe that must be added, or all of life seems to fail and faint along the way. Love is a must if any of us are to survive.

Love is the key to a healthy and happy home. It is the very fabric that makes up the life and hopes and dreams of every child. Without love the child faces a world of confusion and despair. That child's life and mind becomes that of a dry and dull riverbed. Love is just supposed to run through a child's heart. The result is always deadly if there is no love at home.

Kings and queens demand love and loyalty from their subjects. They plead for their kingdom to adore them. Without love in their domain, their rule is void and empty. Love makes the world go round.

Without love one can be alive, but not really be living. One can exist, but not actually enjoy that existence. Love is rudimentary to all existence—It _Is_ Existence!

Wherever there is hate and war and murder and wicked crimes in this earth, it is a direct result of a lack of love and tenderness and care. No matter how tough, mean, and onerous a person can be, or is, deep down inside they are looking for that one, overwhelming, incredible and powerful emotion called love. People bleed for love and to be loved—not just sexual intimacy, but love that holds their hand in difficulties and darkness and even in death.

Real love is more priceless than any diamond on this planet, more valuable than any oil well under the earth, and more powerful than an atomic bomb. God's love changes lives forever. His love is so great and so powerful that even the worst of sinners have been transformed over the centuries. His love is real. Redemptive. I've often thought if I was God and if you were God what would we do, how would we feel about the people and the world we created? What would we think about a beautiful little girl who was murdered in Boulder, Colorado for no apparent reason? And what would we think about some Middle Eastern men who flew airplanes into big, tall buildings and killed several thousand people? How would we feel about people doing so many bad things to other people: bombing one another and raping one another and cheating on each other,   hating each other and even molesting little children and abusing them for the rest of their lives? Could we, would we still love them as the Almighty and want the best for them? Ever think about God's job?

Just think about how powerful our love is for others. You and I are not God, but we can offer so much to so many human beings around us every day in which we live. Through little efforts and big efforts we can do so very much to alleviate the misery and human suffering of others. What an opportunity awaits you and me! When we go out the door, we have that unique window of opportunity to help others, to inspire people's hearts and encourage their lives. Just a phrase or a word or an action can impart love and confidence to others for a lifetime. Yes, love is powerful, very powerful. Thank God He has shown us best how to really love, so much so that He gave His only Son to die for our sins. Give your special love to someone else today. Let God's redemptive love flow through your life into the life of another. Love.

"What a Sweet Shade it is to come under His care!"

HIS SWEET SHADE

You ever take a notion just to do something around the house with no preconceived plan? I do, too. This weekend I cut back some limbs that were in the way of everyone passing by our house. The tree is right next to our sidewalk, so I just got with it and trimmed it back with all the gusto I had.

Later our grandson joined me in picking up the limbs. Now, if you have grandchildren you didn't believe a word I just said. And you're right, too. Davin, six years old, rode his tricycle while "Boppa," as he calls me, picked up those limbs.

As I stood under this gorgeous tree with its thick, lush branches just full of green leaves I heard a little voice speak to me. That voice was the Lord. "You know, Ronnie, this is what I want to be to everyone and to you, too—I want to be your sweet shade."

I could not wait to go to the scriptures to find that Old Testament verse which says, "The Lord is thy keeper: the Lord is thy shade upon thy right hand. The sun shall not smite thee by day, nor the moon by night" (Psalm 121:5, 6).

I kid you not that shade under that tree was unbelievably cool; especially since we've been in a terrible heat wave most of the summer here in colorful Colorado. After living here for fifteen years I do not ever remember this much continuous heat. It's been a doozy. But oh how sweet the shade under this fat, thick, lush tree!

I don't know the difference of temperature that this tree made in the scorching heat of the day, but it was drastic. It was a wonderful drastic, too.

Heat is such a picture of life's tensions and struggles and adversities. In the heat is where we have to make tough decisions. In the heat we require much more strength, and demand much more conditioning. It's an easy walk through life when the road is cool, smooth and easy-going.   But in the heat of things, everything changes. Ask Lance Armstrong, or Tiger Woods, or Marion Jones. They'll tell you that in the heat they're taxed the most and their best skills must come through for them. It's in those pressure-filled, stressful experiences life must go on and we depend upon our greatest resources.

In the end, when our Lord headed to His death, everyone deserted him. All those people who threw their clothes before Him as He entered the city upon a colt which had never been ridden before, all those who praised him and cried "Hosanna to the King," left Him when the heat was on. Peter denied Him. When He was feeding them with the five loaves of bread and the two small fish which the little lad had, it was cool then. Everybody was happy. But in the heat of things, He was alone "he must tread the winepress alone".

What He is saying to you and me is, I want to be your shade. Sweet shade! In the horrible heat of sickness, disappointments, disease, death and deep hurts, I want to be a giant parasol to you.

I stood there for a moment and watched Davin as he rode his little tricycle up the sidewalk in the heat of the day. As I watched him from the cool shade of this big tree, as a grandfather it came home to me even stronger than before, "I want to be a sweet shade to you." We are turning and churning our legs everyday in the sultry heat after another deal, another sale, another success, and another mountain which we want to climb, but we all need a shade now and then. God is that shade. He is that sweet, sweet shade you look for in this desert called life.

The Lord is the place you can find rest and refreshment; that's what a shade does for us. It is the place we can picnic. It is the place we can calm our spirits and our hearts. It is a rehabilitating place for our confidence to grow, a place of recollection and planning. Without rest, without the shade, even the thoroughbred cannot win the race.

David, in his last years upon this earth, after making all the mistakes he did in the heat of the day, sat down and penned those marvelous words, "The Lord is my Shepherd, I shall not want. He makes me to lie down in green pastures; he leads me beside the still waters..." Don't you just sense the canopy? Don't you sense the security and assurance he had come to find in the shade God had provided for him so many times over all his years upon this earth? The only rest he had truly come to know was the rest God had given him.

Yes, I looked at our little grandson and I was reminded so well how God looks at all of us in the heat of the day while He, The Sweet Shade, sees just how bad we need Him and his divine guidance as we tricycle along life's heated highways and schedules. What a Sweet Shade He is to all who come under His care!

"We all need more 'YESs' in our lives."

YES

It really comes to me every so often just how many resources I have within myself; you know, those God-given gifts and "ex tras," if you will, that the Almighty has endowed me with. When my faith begins to wane and my confidence weakens, I am reminded that "With God all things are possible." Also, that "I can do all things through Christ who strengthens me."

I am also reminded that the same God who parted the Red Sea and who raised up His Son from the dead can also raise your life up, your hopes, your dreams, your weak estate and poor condition.

With the Lord you can, you really can, move mountains in your life. Your faith can be as strong as you want it to be. God is sovereign. He is strong. Mighty. Omnipotent. He is the same God who literally lit up Moses' face as He passed by him centuries ago, and Moses only had a look at God's back side.

Is the answer in your faith? No, not just your faith alone. Is it in God and His inexplicable power and awesomness? Where does that most efficient and successful and incredibly fulfilling lifestyle come from? How do you soar in life? I mean really soar? In spite of all the adversity and heartache and disappointment that we can experience down here, just where does your ability come from to be very successful and efficient in your life?

We all need more "YES's!" in our lives. Those "Yes's!" are those experiences where you just know that you know that you are on target with what you are doing. It means you're in the groove. You are making money. You are humming. You are soaring. You are accomplishing what you really want to and intended to. It's when your life is fulfilled. You are happy in what you are doing. No! Not happy, full of joy. So full that each day, yes, that's right, each day you can say with the greatest confidence, YES!

I am convinced that God wants you and me to live in the YES! world. This simply means that everyday you are able to live victoriously enough that there is a deep down YES! written all over your spirit and soul. You may not have to scream it out (i.e., YES!) but you know that it is just there.

We know it because we feel it and experience it. The YES! just exists. And we know that the YES! that is in us is not at the mercy of an argument by someone else because we have experienced it ourselves.

Within you, within me, within all of us is that enormous, limitless power of resources: faith, energy, hope, belief, attitude, creativity and sheer talent coupled with Almighty God to accomplish anything both for God and for humanity and even for ourselves.

Just how great is God? He answered Hannah. He gave her, a barren wife, a new baby. He gave us His only begotten Son to come and actually grace this stage of human life. He was here.

He made you. Me. And this universe and how many more for us to explore? Just how great is God? What is in His pocketbook? What is in His safe? What is in His bank? His barn? What does God own that we can have to help us live? How much will He endow you with to help you build and accomplish what you want to do?

Does God even care about us or our own little world and what we want in this life? Does He really? And if so, then why does He allow so much bad to accompany so much good down here? Also, why does He allow so many people to be so rich, prosper so much, and have so much?

Can God change you? Me? Can He turn things around for us? I mean really turn things around for us? Can He really pull us out of the miry clay and set our feet upon a rock?

I truly believe that in all of us is that incredible power and those limitless resources that He has so aptly endowed us with that anything is possible between us and God. One prayer can reshape your whole world and life. With God there is unbelievable power or He is a liar. You really can count on His Word. You really can move mountains. You really can soar by His great Spirit and strength. He either is. Or, He is not! If He is—and He is, then anything, absolutely anything is possible with Jehovah God.

No matter how puny, small or insignificant your problem God cares. He is a God who "restores." Remember, "He restores my soul." When God is given full reign of your life He is in the business of restitution. He'll put your life back together. Satan seeks to tear you down. But God will build you up again.

The great apostle Paul wrote:

> For this reason we never become discouraged. Even though our physical being is gradually decaying, yet our spiritual being is renewed day by day (11 Corinthians 4:16 TEV).

With God you discover the great value of "Yes's." Seek Him and you'll find your answers.

"Failure is almost always the result of a lack of confidence..."

CONFIDENCE

"**R**on, you've got to have con...dance," his voice trailed away.

"You've got to have what?" I quickly responded.

Again his faint voice, "Con...tence."

His cell phone was not real clear and I was straining to hear his reply.

"You've got to have con..duce," I tried to hear.

"Man! I just can't hear you for some reason."

I was asking my son-in-law who grew up with Tiger Woods, why do I sometimes do so good on some holes in golf and so horribly bad on others?

Finally, Will stopped and made his voice completely and totally clear. "I said, it's all about confidence!...That's what you've gotta have."

"Oh!" I cried out. "Confidence, O.K., I get it now."

"PaPa, we've got to get you a hearing aid," Will finally said in a bit of disgust.

No, it wasn't "con...dance." Nor was it "con...tence." And it sure wasn't "con...duce." It was "confidence!" Boy! When it hit me what Will was really trying to say to me, the word almost knocked me over.

Confidence actually comes from two Latin words: con, meaning together and fidere, which means to trust. My, what a beautiful word when you think about it!

Confidence. That bit of information and conviction given to us in the belief that it will not be passed on. It actually means boldness, and self-reliance. What we learn and practice comes together in a trust within our own beings.

Something takes over that not even the greatest golf pro's can explain when it comes to greatness. It's all in the battle of confidence.

All the practice in the world and all the talent in the world and all the strength in the world will not do unless there's confidence behind the swing of that club.

Just imagine if you and I had more confidence in everything we do. From making those tough sales working with our business clients, speaking in public, to consulting with patients, to dressing for success; what if we had a bit more confidence? What a change this would make in a given day! In our lives!

The super coaches win the big ones because they are able to instill in their players an unusual amount of confidence. Players feel that boldness and self-reliance. They just know they can hit the ball or throw the pass or make the tackle, finish the race or sink that long putt into the hole.

Recently on the front page of the *Wall Street Journal* was an interesting article about how medical and psychiatric people are studying how great golfers can overcome the "yips." The "yips" (choking) come upon the greatest of golfers, and that's why they lose such big tournaments.

It's happened to Palmer, Floyd and Norman and Player and Nicklaus, and yes, even to Tiger Woods, himself. The same is true on the professional women's tour as well. The "yips" are for real!

They cost the pros millions.

You get right up to that two-and-a-half-foot putt and you just miss it. You either push it or pull it, or the ball goes in and comes right back out as it literally swirls around the cup. And you look at that ball and at that cup and say to yourself, "This can't be! Why?"

Everybody in the foursome knows exactly the same feeling. Nobody says anything here either. You just keep your mouth shut if you're smart. 'Cause when you miss this one you don't want any words to come from anyone. Yeah! Cursing isn't the answer either. Why? Think about it. Who are you really cursing? It wasn't the ball or the putter's fault.

Failure is almost always the result of a lack of confidence and a lot of distrust, whether it is in yourself or in others.

Confidence! It takes a lot of this to run a nation, a business, a home, a family, a ball club, a team, an army, a church, a school, a hospital, and a government. Things just don't always run by themselves. Believing in yourself and in God and in your staff or business associates is huge when it comes to success.

Probably one of the greatest statements ever recorded about confidence was when the Apostle Paul declared, "I can do all things through Christ who strengthens me." (Philippians 4:19) Wow! What self-assurance and boldness! I can! I can! I can! That's where it begins and then when we lean upon the Master, I can through Him and His great resources of strength and power do all things.

What a bold, bold statement! "I can do all things through Christ who strengthens me." Now that's confidence, and it's confidence in the right Person, too.

"He (Christ) wants to salvage our past and us as well."

REGRETS

He was very old, sitting there on his simple bed in a simple room inside a very simple little house. He was talking to a young man about his many years as a minister in Memphis and throughout the world, a very famous minister at that. The young man, a friend of mine many years ago, said he just had to go and visit the retired and ailing R. G. Lee before the Lord took him home. Good thing, too, because Dr. Lee died not too long afterwards.

Here was a man who could have retired in luxury; he could have lived wherever he wanted. He could have had just about anything he wanted as well. However, he chose to go out with just about what he had when he entered this big world from his beginning.

He did, however, leave behind many books he had authored, and his masterpiece sermon, **Payday Someday**. I heard him preach it when I was very young, and I, too, found myself one of many thousands over the years who were totally spellbound by his message.

A little over a year ago I was stunned that my brother-in-law somehow had come across a taped copy of this incredible sermon. As I listened to the words pour out of the mouth of this giant preacher and speaker I could visualize him standing before me so many years earlier. I forget just how many times he preached this famous message, but it was worth counting, believe me.

I remember also that awful murderous woman, Tony Jo Henry, who had murdered and mangled the man she went to death row over. She actually tortured him, as I recall—a heinous crime to say the least.

Dr. Lee dramatized, by the slap of his hands, Tony Jo's walk to her death chamber the day she was executed. He also relates when she is asked why she did it, and the evil-hearted soul declares, "I knew God was in control all the time; I just wanted to steal one little act from him."

Do you have regrets? Do you look back over your shoulder and ask yourself sometime, "If only I had it to do over again?" I'm sure you do. I know I do. We don't have to kill a person just to regret our past. We can carry one small skeleton in our closet and still try "to steal one little act from God."

As a senior now, I look back over my shoulder more and more and wonder about those things I wish I had changed, but neither I nor you can recall yesterday. Today is not only the first day of the rest of our lives, it is the only day past yesterday. Yesterday is irrecoverable, and irreplaceable.

Surely this is why the Psalmist declared, "Weeping may endure for a night, but joy comes in the morning" (Psalm 30:5 NKJV). The night here, to me, represents the past. David saw Bathsheba and killed for her. He loved her more than himself and anyone else and his God in moments of passion and foolishness. And it cost him his kingdom, his family, his future, and his child with Bathsheba.

In his deepest regrets, David could only look back at that nighttime period in his life where he saw weeping and anguish of his soul for such a stupid, silly, sinful and selfish mistake. The hurt was so deep and so despairing that he could best describe it as, "Weeping may endure for a night..."

Upon his bed he lived with the blood of Uriah on his hands. This was Bathsheba's husband. There were not enough tears to express his guilt and his regret. And yet, somehow, some way, God brought him out of his miry clay and set his feet upon a rock and re-did David's heart. The great grace and mercy and sheer power of God loosed David from his dark night of tears into a morning of joy. So much so that Daivd could actually say, "Weeping may endure for a night, but joy comes in the morning."

No matter how black your night is, no matter how dreary your past has been, with all of your mistakes and hates, with all of your losses and crosses, we can be sure that joy comes in the morning. We have a God who can erase our past, blot out our wrongs, forgive us, restore us and change us for all eternity.

Dr. Lee was truly the Prince of preachers. He told us about a lady who thought she would steal just one little act from God's play called life. But she didn't. In the end she went to her death knowing full well that she could only die with regrets. Remember she said, "I just wanted to steal..." She knew she never really did. Someone penned so well:

How I wish there was some wonderful place called the Land of Beginning Again,
Where all our heartaches and all our mistakes and all our poor selfish griefs...
Could be dropped like a shabby old coat at the door,
And never be put on again.

Thank God we can drop those regrets at the door of the cross of Christ.

You and I can live in freedom if we want to. Christ paid an awful price for forgiveness. He wants to salvage our past and us as well.

Whatever we've done in the past is over, and whatever consequences we must face we can with the Lord helping us. "If God is for us, who can be against us?" Not even the darkest, most bitter night of weeping can defeat us, because "Joy really does come in the morning."

GIVING THANKS

"Music stirs the soul and moves the spirit."

EVERY MORNING

"Sing David," I would ask as a kid. Every morning as we would jump into that stinking ditch I would bug him to start singing. Yeah! I remember now. I would even beg him at times.

He was a young man, a young African American man with the voice of a bird. My dad owned a plumbing company. And we were laying pipe for a sewer line on a pretty big project.

Every summer I worked with David and Jake. It seemed for years as I think back now. They were both African Americans. Of course, in the South this was kind of unheard of in the sixties, a boss's son hanging around black folk. But I did and I loved those guys and loved to work with them. They loved me.

Jake would bring the best coffee you've ever tasted. Wow, was it good! He always added a little cream and just a touch of sugar. I can still see us now digging in that muddy clay-filled ditch over our heads. Even the awful smell of that earth comes back to me at times, so real that I feel like I've stepped back into the hole. But then, there was Jake's special blend to get us through those hot, humid summer days; Starbucks would have died for such a blend today.

David was a tall, handsome young man. He had the prettiest white teeth, too. There was no choir behind him, or band or instruments, just his voice that filled that ditch and the heavens above us. His voice now lingers in my memory and seems to be so surreal. How he could sing! He had a voice of a bird that would "send" anyone's soul soaring and such a dynamic personality to go with it. He seemed to be all smiles in such a dirty, nasty environment.

When I think of those days I think of scripture where the Lamentation says, "His mercies are new every morning and great is His faithfulness." Even in the depths of a sewer ditch, in the stench of the muddy earth, I was so blessed and refreshed and stirred by the voice of a bird, by David singing about the Lord and His greatness. Oh! If it could have only been taped; well, you're right, it is taped in the memory of this mind after almost forty years now.

Music stirs the soul and moves our spirits. It is a gift. It is one of those many mercies from God in heaven. And I, well, I was so blessed by hearing such an incredible voice as a teenager long ago.

I don't know what happened to David. My dad told me sometime back that Jake died. Who knows, David just may be singing to Jake on the steps of their mansions in heaven for all I know. As I reminisce today I can only be thankful for two black angels that God sent my way. And of all places to meet them and their sweet spirits, beautiful voices and delicious coffee was in a dark, deep sewer ditch in Southeast Texas. Thank you, Father, for those mercies that you give to us every morning.

"... the face is peaceful when the faith is powerful."

HOW BLESSED WE ARE

I read about a man in Europe who had been blind his entire life; better than fifty years. A surgeon informed him that he thought it was possible, at least a small chance, he might be able to see again. The man didn't have a lot of faith, but he was willing to undergo the surgery.

After the procedure that great surgeon came in and helped the nurse unwrap the bandages. The man was almost afraid at first to open his eyes for fear the surgery was a failure. However, he thought to himself, "I might as well face the truth. If I'm still blind nothing has changed. If it worked, I'll be the happiest person on this planet."

So he opened his eyes. For a moment he saw nothing. Then his blurred vision turned into clearer and clearer scenes of people around his bedside.

"My God," he exclaimed, "I can see, I can see! It worked...it worked...I can really see for the first time in my life."

After some time passed, this man came back to see his surgeon. Dr. Endicott asked the man, "John, what has impressed you the most since you've been able to see?"

"Well, Doc," John replied, "I cannot believe the sadness I see on so many human faces. I just never realized how troubled my human race really is. This is what's impressed me the most, this sadness and gloom."

When I read this story sometime ago, I thought what a tragedy. Here a man who could finally see after all those years, saw something he wished he was blind to again. It is obvious to me that the face is peaceful when the faith is powerful. So many people have never discovered the power of faith, faith in God that can change everything.

Only recently I saw an old couple walking across the street in downtown Denver. The old man had on those old, ugly and dirty polyester pants. He and his wife looked so poor and so broken. It looked like life had dished them every bitter pill it had. I know what you're thinking, they probably own a skyscraper in downtown Denver—and they might.

But I don't think so. They looked so very pitiful. And yet, I thought to myself. "How many people have big homes and big cars and big bank accounts and yet they have no peace inside them?" They are a part of the same human race who were so sad that the once blind man saw.

Some things we just can't hide. When we're sick, it shows on our face. When we've lost our job, it shows on our face. When we've lost a loved one or friend, it shows on our face. And the same is true when success comes and everything goes right; it shows, too.

Remember when Moses came down from the mountain, he had been privileged to see the back side of God? His face lit up like the sun. The Hebrew children were literally afraid of him because his face shined so. Finally, Moses placed a veil upon his face.

Wow! That must have been some experience for Moses. What God did in his heart, it showed on his face. The same can be true for you and me as well. The closer we get to the Lord, the more our own countenance will change. The status of the heart always shows in the expression of one's face.

Whatever you have, whatever gifts and talents God has endowed you with just remember "how blessed we are."

"Really we are all in a hut."

THE HUT

There really are no words to describe some things in life. You know, you just look at some things that exist here and you wonder, and wonder some more, and ask yourself, "Why?" Or, ask, "How can this be?"

Along the Eastern side of the Central American Border in the Caribbean Sea there is a hut that sits out on the waters. A family lives there as I write these words. The hut is sort of out on a peninsula. In fact, it sits right at the end of the peninsula, except it really is out on the water, just beyond the point of the peninsula. It looks so alone in such a vast sea of water. It looks so vulnerable to nature's cruel and merciless storms, too.

But there it sits; draped with a décor of nets and poles, of fishing tackle and household necessities. Boards, poles, and other stuff make up the landscape, or I should say seascape.

The waters around the hut are to die for. Their beautiful aqua colors and spectacular scenery is a slice of heaven itself. Yet, right there in the midst of this incredible picture of brilliance and breathtaking tropical paradise is a hut—somebody's home.

For most of us we would only pity such poor people on this planet, but it's their home. It's where they wake up every morning. It's where their children grow up and fish and learn about life. It's about people and about the world around them. But for the modern urban family this would be the last place on earth that they would be able to cope with life and all of its exigencies.

I've seen this hut. It is forever in my mind and soul. It is out there at the point of that peninsula all by itself. There is not another hut in sight. Those people living there have the whole ocean and world to themselves it seems. But that little hut, I simply cannot erase it from my mind; I think about it often since I saw it earlier this year while teaching on a cruise.

You can tell that everything they own is handmade. Nothing is fancy. It is so simple. It appears so "unstable." Surely they pay no taxes on such a hut. Or, do they? I don't know. And I'm sure that's not a concern to them at all. It looks like they are just living, and for some reason I don't think they have a care in the world compared to people like you and me here in the States.

But Oh those waters! There is not a writer on this earth that could ever pen such a breathtaking view. The shades of green and blue and turquoise were the prettiest I personally have ever seen before. This hut, this tiny little place on the face of the earth, was surrounded with a carpet of iridescent waters. Those pristine waters were so lovely, so commanding you just have to go back to them; they are that captivating.

Who are they? Who were they? Best I don't know I'm sure. I'd love to sit down with them and find out about their lives, some of the history that brought them to such a place. Are they a second generation or fourth or fifth generation that has weathered the storms and the tropical sun and humid days for decades, or for centuries? Who knows, really?

In a hut upon a sea, that says it all I guess. It left an indelible print upon this author's mind and life.

The wisest man who ever lived once wrote, "For who knows what is good for a man in life, during the few and meaningless days he passes through like a shadow? Who can tell him what will happen under the sun after he is gone?" (Ecclesiastes 6:12 KJV).

Really, we are all in a hut. Some are just more expensive and colorful and larger and fancier and warmer and cooler and nicer and maybe even safer than others. But when all is said and done it's where we lay our heads at night for rest and sleep and where we make a hut (house) a home.

What a scene upon the sea! Can you even imagine getting up and just jumping into the warm waters and taking a fresh morning swim before breakfast every day of your life if you chose to? Wow! And a fat flounder comes by, and you just spear him and roast him for dinner that night. Unbelievable! Huh?

Oh! You can be sure you don't have to worry about hair spray or cologne or some name-brand garment there; nobody gives a flip.

The dictionary says a hut is a crude or makeshift dwelling; a shack. Well, that's what I saw that day in the Caribbean Sea in Central America. No doubt about it. But it saw me more than I saw it— get my drift?

Since I saw that little hut in the sea I truly have been more grateful than ever before for the countless blessings that God has bestowed upon me and my family and this great country we call the USA. "It saw me." Poor English I know. But that little hut spoke more sermons to me than a preacher could say in a whole year.

It said, "Look at me, Ronnie. Take a real good look at me and remember where you live and what you have and what your gra- cious God has blessed you with so abundantly; take a real, good, long, look while you can. And the next time you find yourself complaining about running out of bread or milk or having a bad hair day or having to deal with conjested traffic, or all these other little annoyances just remember me, The Hut."

And I have.

"God's tongue is in His creation itself."

THE WAY WE WORK

O nly now and then does life afford us such timeless drama and magical scenes as I witnessed yesterday. It was supposed to be just another dinner out with my wife and son, which we do occasionally. But it did not work that way. In fact, it became in my estimation, a special gift from God.

As I pushed my handicapped wife up the inclines which I am now starting to get used to, I looked out of the restaurant window sometime later and saw a young lady go flying by us in an electric wheel chair. She, too, was coming into the same restaurant. She had no legs. I know because she came into the same dining room we were in, the handicapped area. It wasn't until my wife, Nancy Jean, became temporarily handicapped that I've come to understand why all the handicapped people want so many laws changed in this country. They really are denied some of the most basic rights and privileges that able-bodied people take for granted.

As Jason, our son, Nancy Jean and I sat there for a while eating and visiting together I could not help but sense the continuous movement of something out of the corner of my eye. For some time I never paid much attention, but as the evening wore on I finally turned and noticed a table of six or eight people, all adults, speaking via sign language. Every now and then I could not help but give an extra glance in the restaurant's handicap section at all these adult people speaking through such artistic hand movement.

I am no sign language person, definitely not a pro at it, but these people had done this awhile one could tell. As I sat there listening to Nancy Jean and Jason talk, I could not help but say a silent prayer in my heart and thank God for my legs and my feet and ears and my tongue. This unusual instrument in our mouths which helps us to eat and speak and taste and give our doctor signs of health, is a masterpiece which our Heavenly Father and Creator constructed.

Magic, that's what it was. We talked and they used their hands to communicate the same words in their conversation. And the table was so quiet next to us, except for the rattling of a dish or fork now and then. They smiled and conversed and enjoyed their dinner just like we did, maybe even more, for all that I know.

We often refer to God and His greatness for human creation. It is incredible how He gave us eyes to see with and a heart to pump the flow of life-blood within our bodies, but what about our tongues? Wow! What an instrument He designed there. We use this every day in some way in our work and in our play. And for those of us who are not handicapped by speech, we employ our tongue daily as much or more than any other instrument in our bodies.

For some, of course, they never give it a rest. It is no wonder the scriptures teach us how much trouble the tongue can become when it slams others with destructive criticism. James compares the tongue with a bit in a horse's mouth, or like a small rudder on a great ship. Both can steer greatness of power to be so little. James writes:

And the tongue is a fire, a world of iniquity: The tongue is so set among our members, that it defiles the whole body, and sets on fire the course of nature; and it is set on fire by hell (James 3:6 NKJV).

My, how mixed up we are down here on this planet! Hollywood has taught us that one must be pretty, well-figured, smart, a super star, popular, dynamic, charming, and famous to be somebody on this planet. This is why I am so glad a young lady became Miss America some years ago even though she was deaf. Heather Whitestone McCallum was the first woman with a disability to be crowned Miss America (1995). Heather became deaf when she was eighteen months old.

I'm not sure we will ever get it. The way we work and the way God works are almost never the same. It is no wonder the Psalmist wrote centuries ago, "The heavens declare the glory of God; and the firmament shows His handywork. Day unto day utters speech,

and night unto night shows knowledge" (Psalm 19:1,2).
God's tongue is in His creation itself. Look around you and listen, because He is speaking to you loud and clear every pithy way and day He can. "Day unto day utters speech," Wow! And on this day and in this restaurant and at this table God uttered a loud speech into my heart, one I shall never forget. He reminded me of how blessed we are just to be able to talk, to communicate freely. He reminded me that the way we work, the way we get along down here demands our own creativity and energy and enthusiasm.

No matter who you are, you have a gift to share, a heart to love with and a tongue (or hands) to communicate with to praise your Creator and Savior and those you love. The Psalmist was so taken by this I think this is why he declared, "Bless the Lord O my soul; and all that is within me, bless His holy name" (Psalm 103:1). Sing a song of praise to Him today. Use your tongue. Use your hands. He is <u>worthy</u> of your praise. He is worthy of our praise.

"Good coaching is always good news."

THE COACH

It was the most perfect day of the year. A cool snap had come through, and the fall day was the most picturesque day you could ever imagine. After a rush of a morning, I decided to steal a few hours of the day on the golf course. The trees, of course, were taking their bow in the sun with their gorgeous colors.

I was coming up the course to the sixth hole. I was playing absolutely horrible, too. I was beginning to wonder if I had ever hit a golf ball before; ever feel that way? In and out of the sand traps, in the rough, poor chip shots and one GIR (greens in regulation) after five holes. I was getting more and more angry at myself, but I kept playing. I do believe, though, it was the worst playing I've done in years—inexcusable to say the least!

After chipping in the sand trap more than once on the sixth, I noticed someone had left their sand wedge upon the green. For a split second I actually wondered if God was starting to feel sorry for me and just maybe He placed a magic sand wedge there to help me get onto the green. Guess what? I used it and made an almost perfect shot, too.

As I drove my cart up to the seventh hole I noticed an old gentleman looking frantically through his set of clubs. He was scratching his head and talking to his other two partners.

"Hey!" I cried, "This wouldn't be yours would it?"

"Hey!" he cried back, "I've been looking for that.....thanks a million."

I sat there alone for just a few seconds and then he and his partners began to introduce themselves to me. Finally, one of the older men blurted, "You playing with anyone?"

"No."

"Well, how about playing with us the rest of the day?" The voice trailed away.

"OK, sure, I'd be honored," muttering to myself, "dear God! You guys don't know what you're in for the rest of the day."

Little did I know why the Lord allowed all of this to happen; only after the game was over did it really hit me.

I'll just use the name, Babe. In that foursome was a former pro football player and coach who has played many games of golf. And undoubtedly he saw something good in me because he spent the rest of the afternoon coaching me and giving me tips to improve my game. As the day wore on, I finally called Babe over and showed him the incredible difference between my first nine and my last nine holes on my score card. It was like I had been converted.

It was a miracle! At least to me it was. Babe said that I hit one drive longer than he'd ever seen on number seventeen. Man, did that make me feel good!

But the truth; what is truth? The truth this day was that I was the student and Babe was the coach. And I can truthfully say that I listened and he taught.

It's been a couple of years ago when I heard Tiger Woods say that he really needed to get back to Houston. He was being interviewed, and the newscaster was drilling him on his inconsistent drives. Tiger was having a bad tournament, a rare thing, I know. But he blurted out, "I really need to see my coach in Houston. I've just got to get back down there."

If Tiger Woods needs a coach, how much more do you...and I.

Remember in scriptures that man, that Ethiopian eunuch? He was an important official in charge of all the treasury of Candace, queen of the Ethiopians. He was on a chariot ride on his way back from Jerusalem where he had gone to worship. But he was perplexed because he was reading in Isaiah verses which he did not understand. He was in a sand trap trying to get out.

And along came Philip, the coach, who was led of God to meet this man in a desert. It's no fun being in a sand trap. I don't care who you are, it's just no fun.

Philip: "Do you understand what you are reading?"

The Ethiopian eunuch responded, "How can I understand unless someone explains it to me?"

Then the coaching began. Get your head behind the ball. Swing all the way through. Relax. It's only a game; get rid of the stress! Bend your knees a little. Keep that left arm straight as you come back with the club.

Philip (the coach long ago), began with that very passage of Scripture and told him the good news about Jesus.

Good coaching is always good news. Great players have had great coaches. Great players are greatly coachable. A hint here, and a tip there, and a lot of practice and more coaching, and you're on your way to success and victories.

What a memorable day this was in my life! Thanks Coach.

It really is amazing what one or two ideas can do to make a drastic change for good in all our lives. My wife has taught school most of her adult life. Boy! What a coach she's been, too. She's been a coach to young, bendable, educable minds and lives. I'm not surprised that one year she was named teacher of the year at her elementary school. Great coaches are dedicated. They're thinking ahead when no one else is in the game, no one else is in the class.

The greatest Coach who ever lived taught us how to live and how to die. He did such a masterful coaching job with his twelve players that this world has never been the same and never will be again.

What a Coach! And even in His dying moments He still coached:

> To His mother, "Dear woman, here is your son," and to the disciple, John, "Here is your mother." From that time on, this disciple took her into his home.

There's something about the eyes of a great coach. You sense the possibility that they see in you with those piercing eyes. I could see it in Babe's. Can you imagine how it was to look into the eyes of Almighty God incarnate (in the person of a human being)? This Jesus must have had eyes that cut through the soul itself. When He looked at you, you listened, too. That's why Judas could not cope with his betrayal of the lovely Christ. Those eyes of his Coach were just too much to reckon with in the end, so he killed himself out of guilt and fear. Wow! What piercing eyes can do to a person in the end!

The beautiful, perfect, fall day came to close on the old golf course, but a brand new swing opened up for me. And as we parted, I gave the old coach a tube of Titlelist golf balls and said, "Thank you Coach. You've made my day and changed my entire game. See you down the road, Lord willing." And we walked away from each other, both refreshed. I knew I had been with a great coach.

PRAYER

"Winning and prayer, they go hand-in-hand."

WINNING THROUGH PRAYER

William James, the great psychologist, said, "You can change your life by altering the attitude of your mind." And the way you and I do this is through prayer. God is our source of power. The reason you live in any kind of "bind" is because of a missing link in prayer between you and God.

Prayer is the key which opens and closes doors for your life. Often God needs to close a door for us rather than open it. You weaken your prayer skills and efficiency by failing to realize just how much you can win through prayer. There is nothing wrong with winning, either.

As I get older and think more about God and all of His awesome ways and creation and resources, I think, who are we kidding? God is a mega winner. He's built a whole universe and endless others. There is no end to Him or His ownership and control. If somebody's got that much stuff and savvy and sovereignty, I think you and I can call Him a winner.

By the way, when I allude to winning I mean "getting the job done." I think you would agree that God "Gets His jobs done." That's what winning is all about. A coach can brag all about those fans that he wants to at the end of a major championship, but if he and that team don't get the job done those same fans will send him "packing."

Prayer works. Although you kneel and pray and think God is a million miles away and you feel like you're talking into the air itself, you're not. He is right there with you as a believer. He is hearing you, He is listening to you, and He cares about your hurting heart.

I shall never forget Bobby Mankin with whom I went to college. He had shot up his body with drugs so much that he finally had to inject the heroin underneath his toenails because he had no more veins in his arms for the injections. Bobby told me one night, "Ronnie, I came to the point in my life that I just said, 'God if you can help me, if you can change my life and my heart, I'm asking you to save my soul.'"

It just so happened that God could, and He did. God changed a drug addict into one of the greatest modern-day witnesses I have ever known or met. Bobby Mankin touched thousands of lives before his untimely death in an auto accident. But Bobby would never have touched anyone's life if it had not been for him winning through prayer.

We as a nation can brag all we want about our military might and superiority as a super power, but without prayer we would be nothing. Prayer has won the recent Iraqi war, not just military force. When and if God withholds His mighty hand from America we will lose in war. All the bombs and warheads on this earth cannot compete with Almighty God's omnipotence.

Christ, in all of His glory and potential power here on earth, submitted to prayer constantly because He, too, wanted to win through prayer—and He did. His entire life was spent on the go, never stopping: in mountains, on the sea, in wildernesses, in towns and communities. People sought Him because they knew He had something they didn't. They also sought Him because they found a source of healing. He was a winner to them. This is why you read in Mark:

And wheresoever He entered, into villages, or cities, or country, they laid the sick in the streets, and besought Him that they might touch if it were but the border of His garment: and as many as touched Him were made whole (St. Mark 6:56 RKJV).

I don't know what your heartache, or personal challenge is that you are facing, but no matter what you're going through right now, you win through prayer. If it is a health problem, a betrayal by a business associate, divorce, or dealing with a difficult family member, prayer is your answer. Prayer will get you across the finish line. The very thing that's bugging you most can be defeated through your personal intercession with the King. When you touch the border of His garment healing is on the way. He didn't go to the cross just for the fun of it or to make a name for Himself; "by His stripes we are healed" (we win).

Winning and prayer, they go hand-in-hand. Yes, sometimes God will allow you to lose no matter how hard and sincere you may pray. But when all is said and done through prayer you will always come out on top in the end. Somehow God just makes everything to dovetail and fall into place, even in the worst of disasters. Remember: "On your knee is the key."

"... (People) need to know that our Lord has prayed for us..."

SIX MOST POWERFUL WORDS
Dr. Luke's Red Letter Edition

My long-time pastor and friend, the late Rev. W. W. Kennedy, used to have a morning radio program in South east Texas. He would always begin his program with that marvelous prayer by Cardinal Ralph Cushman. Perhaps you've heard it, too.

I met God in the morning,
When my day was at its best;
His presence came like the sunrise,
Like a glory in my breast.

All day long His presence lingered,
All day long He stayed with me;
And we sailed in perfect calmness,
Over a very troubled sea.

Other ships were blown and battered,
Other ships were sore distressed;
But the winds that seem to drive them,
Brought to us a peace and rest.

So I think I know the secret.
Learned from many a troubled way;
You must seek Him in the morning.
If you want Him through the day.

This prayer I say almost every morning even to this day after some forty years since I first heard it. Prayer is such a wonderful way to live and to experience our relationship with the Almighty.

I personally feel that prayer by most of us is viewed too much as a source of power. As I have gotten older prayer has become more of a declaration first; at least to me it has.

When we talk to Him, we are acknowledging His greatness. To bow to God is, to me, acknowledging Him as the Sovereign God of all existence, our Ruler and King. So when I pray and you pray we are in every way making a real declaration to the most Awesome One. We are praying to "Suigeneris," which means He is of His own kind—there is no other, or equal.

And second, prayer, to me, is a communication of total dependence on the One who has the strength and guidance to help us through our struggles. We can't. But He can. We are, you might say, "leaners." And this does not diminish our own potentials and abilities. We are weak, He is strong. We are human, He is Almighty; so you and I lean upon Him to get us through the rough seas of life.

And third, prayer, to me, is that constant reminder that I am the creature walking down here with my Creator and Father and Maker and Savior. As I talk to Him in prayer that is how I commune with Him. He is as real as the palm of our hand. You and I are the beings He made and fashioned for His purposes. And you and I know Him through the gift of His only Son, Jesus, who came to this earth as a creature just like we did, except His birth was divine.

It is my sincere belief that most prayers today are offered with an attitude that they want to get from God rather than allow God to give to them—there is a difference. This is why the Jabez Prayer Book took this nation by storm. People are almost entranced by wanting to get power and blessings and prosperity and healing and what I call, JPS (Just Plain Stuff) from God. This way they are working to receive something from God. And I believe God is capable of doing all of these things.

However, real prayer is simply allowing God to do His thing in us;

I believe it's Him at work, not us.

My assistant recently called out to me, "Ronnie, you have an old friend on the line holding for you!"

I picked up the phone and it was the Prophet — in fact, the only modern day prophet I know of in today's computerized world. I call him the Prophet because of his deep, deep thought and intense relationship with the Lord. I have often referred to him over the years in my writings.

> "Ron," he began, "please read over there in Dr. Luke's Red Letter Edition the Six Most Powerful Words that I think the Lord spoke over His lifetime. You'll find it in Luke 22:32. You know, he was a real physician back then."

And then he changed the subject and started asking me about Long Term Care insurance issues. When the Prophet gives me a verse I don't race to a copy of the scriptures and hurriedly read it. Never! I want to ingest it, digest it and digest it some more before I try to assimilate it in my mind and heart and soul, and before I allow the Holy Spirit to make it come alive within me. He feeds me. It is so good and so deep I like to chew on it a long time.

So later in the evening I came home and started reading and study-ing what he had pointed out to me. Wow! I can't get it out of my mind. I don't want to get it out of my mind. What comforting words! What new assurance it has brought me and what it will bring to you, my reader.

It struck such a deep chord within me that I had to call the Prophet back the next day and see where he was coming from. My son and I looked at it from every angle we could. And even my son got excited about what the Prophet must have been saying, and seeing, and interpreting in these Six Most Powerful Words Christ ever spoke. (Have you looked yet? I can't blame you.)

"Joe," I asked, "what was your take on what He said, 'But, I have prayed for you?'"

"It is past tense, Ron." And then he allowed a time of quietness to come about on the phone. Wow! I thought to myself, that's right. And then he spoke and I listened.

"Ron, that was the darkest hour of Peter's life. You know he had heard the rumors and critics' vows to kill Jesus. It was all about to come to an end. Jesus had said enough about His death to Peter and the Twelve that he knew the end was very near.

"What's so incredible here is that the Lord had already prayed for Simon Peter; finished, over with. He knew that Simon Peter, just like us, was capable of being sifted like wheat...you know that can happen to all of us; it does sometimes, too.

"Remember this, Ronnie, when the Lord prayed, it went right to the Throne of Grace, too.

"We're used to those basketball prayers. You know, the kind that bounce off the ceiling and the floor and the walls and never get to that Throne. Well, this one didn't bounce off anything. It landed in the heart of God's throne of grace.

"By the way, Ronnie, these modern-day theologians and Bible scholars who don't believe that we can put our names now where Peter's was...you know, in scripture, and that the Lord can't pray for us, too; you can be sure they've never been to the cross. This verse is for me and you and everybody else that is looking for such comfort.

"No. He doesn't want my faith or your faith or anyone else's faith to fail either. He wants us to strengthen each other, just like He did old Simon."

"Joe," with tears in my eyes I said, "you are exactly right. People out there in this world of so much complexity and confusion need to know that our Lord has prayed for us—past tense. He does care about us, even though sometime we think He has forgotten about us. And in reality He is, through His caring Spirit, in fact praying for us with all of our problems which we are facing every day. Man! What assurance!"

"That's right, Ron...that's right..." the Prophet's voice trailed off.

So today when you talk to Him, just remember. He's already been up praying for you and for me that our faith will not be sifted, will not be weakened or defeated. Whatever you're facing this day in your life, you are not alone, nor are you praying by yourself. What a promise of scripture for you!

And I hope you can say as Cardinal Cushman...I really did meet God in the morning when my day was at its best...

HOME

"He is the Master Builder."

MAKE BELIEVE

Just another Friday evening, I thought, as I drove quickly to pick up our six-year-old grandson. I had just spoken to a religious board meeting about our seminars which we conduct on charitable giving.

So I decided to run by and pick up Dal, as we call him. After scurrying along he and I got everything into the car and attached one of those infamous car seats that always give grandparents a headache when they have to be installed. We were all ready for the trip home: backpack, snack, car seat, a favorite toy and me and Dal. Off we went. Zoom!

Here I've just spoken to leading professionals and church leaders across the state of Colorado. Now I've shifted my mind to a six-year-old and all his needs, wants and wishes.

We're just puttering down the road and Dal makes a huge declaration: "Boppa," as he calls me, "when I get to be a big kid I'm gonna build a big house for God and everybody else so we can all live down here together."

"Really?" I replied.

"Yep," Dal continued confidently, "And Pugsley (our late Boston Terrier who died this year) and my daddy's daddy and Nanna's mother and daddy and everybody will get to live down here. They won't even have to go to heaven."

"Wow!" I replied again. "But where are you going to build it?"

"We just passed it, Boppa."

"Oh! We did?"

"Yeah, right back there was some land for sale."

At this point this is just unbelievable—I begin to think I'm just hearing things; after all this is just a little kid talking.

"OK," I conceded.

"And Boppa," (He's really wound up by this time now)... "God's house is not going to have a single door or window in it."

"Well, why not, Dal?" I asked (because this was getting very interesting to me).

"Cause, Boppa," he explained in his speech to this one grandparent board member, "Don't you know God is invisible? He can just walk right through the walls. He doesn't need a door to walk through, nor a window."

By this time I am so taken by this child's **make believe** that I am overwhelmed by his sincerity and purity of heart. And what a thought!

"Well, Dal that would be wonderful. I mean, just wonderful. And like you say, 'We can just all live together down here and be one big family.'"

"That's right, Boppa. I can't wait 'til I get big so I can build a big house for God and all His people."

No heaven, we'll just all live together down here. But then, that is heaven. In the mind of my grandson he was actually describing heaven to me and did not realize it. Remember, "the meek shall inherit the earth?" The only difference, of course, is we know who is building the house for God. He is the **Master Builder**.

In my Father's house are many mansions: if it were not so, I would have told you. I go to prepare a place for you. And if I go and prepare a place for you, I will come again, and receive you unto myself; that where I am, there you may be also (St. John 14:2, 3 RKJV).

Make believe. I think we were all good at that growing up. Reality sets in, however, when we get a little older and all those tough, bad things happen in life that we were never expecting. Then, we start looking through our eyes with new perspectives. We realize how real war is, and death and disappointments and job losses and divorces and all the other **bad stuff** that we encounter.

We also come to that realization that some things we just don't have control over. And other things we can't possibly understand because they are just not to be understood, at least not in this life. But from my grandson's point of view he had it all figured out and I am glad.

Dal's heaven is where there is no parting. We're just one big happy family, under one big roof, with one big God and everybody's all together.

Jump over into scripture and you'll read something very similar to Dal's make believe heaven:

> And I saw a new heaven and a new earth: for the first heaven and the first earth were passed away; and there was no more sea.

> And I, John, saw the holy city, New Jerusalem, coming down from God out of heaven, prepared as a bride adorned for her husband.

> And I heard a great voice out of heaven saying, Behold the tabernacle of God is with men, and he will dwell with them, and they shall be his people, and God himself shall be with them, and be their God.

And God shall wipe away all tears from their eyes; and there shall be no more death, neither sorrow, nor crying, neither shall there be any more pain: for the former things are passed away. (Revelation 21:1-4 KJV).

I never told my grandson that his dream could never be. I like make believe myself. I still like to dream. I like to look into the starry-filled night and think about God and all of his greatness and handiwork. I like to think about what could be; I resist reality. Yeah! I know that's not good sometimes; in fact, most of the time. But I'm a dreamer, too.

I love those lines of the Psalmist:

> The heavens declare the glory of God; and the firmament shows his handiwork
>
> Day unto day utters speech, and night unto night shows knowledge.(Psalm 19:1,2 KJV).

Dal showed his Boppa a lot of knowledge this night from a six-year-old mind. We got home and Dal started performing more **make believe** in front of us with a puppet show. We were in the background and all the stuffed animals had front row tickets. He put on a great performance. It was all real, too, and some real **make believe**, as well. What a fantastic night to remember!

And just think, No! just listen. He's hammering together a door on your mansion right now and waiting for you and me to get there.

"What do you own up there?"

MY HOUSE,
THE OLD HOME PLACE

There are not enough descriptive words or even definitive reasons to explain why a house is more than just a building to some people. I've always heard that a house and a home are not the same; I believe this to some degree, too. A house is more of the building, while a home is more of the family (blood, sweat and tears, values and virtues) inside this building.

However, as I am getting older I have come to realize, too, that a house and a person, a house and the family, a house and anybody, seem to be literally fused together over time. Most of my father's family have the same painting of what we have always called "the old home place" in deep East Texas. We had an artist friend draw "the old home place" on a canvas years ago. This old home place is in the community of Jericho, Texas, which is just a few miles north of Center, Texas.

"The old home place" was really just a very simple frame house with a tin roof on top of it and a reddish brick fireplace stack. But "the old home place" became synonymous with the Johnson family over the decades. And to this day we all still refer to "the old home place" when we are talking about the past. Now that building represented something. In fact, I'm convinced that a house becomes to some families more than just a construction of wood and glass and steel and bricks and building stuff. It becomes them. At this place (your house) and within those walls there is fusion. Something mysterious takes place which, as I said in the beginning, cannot be described or defined with mere words.

Over the years I have been privileged to visit every kind of house and dwelling you could imagine. From Mexico to the Middle East, from Europe to Africa, from the good ole USA to foreign islands,

I have been the guest of mud huts, palaces, ranches, mansions, high rise apartments, town houses, mobile homes, tents, hotels, motels, ships, dormitories, duplexes, houseboats, lodges, penthouses, shacks, castle, and encampments. But as I look back now I realize more than ever that in all of those places people are still the same; they need a place to rest and lay their heads at night for the next day's work.

The Lord promised when he was upon this earth, "In my Father's house are many mansions, if it were not so I would have told you…I go to prepare a place for you that where I am there you may be also…" Goodness, just think. One day we will be housed in the home of the Master builder. What an incredible thought! We just think we've seen a beautiful home or mansion down here.

I remember as a pastor I used to tell the story of the young preacher who was visiting a very wealthy rancher in his community. The rancher knew everything there is to know about ranching, but his wife and family could not get him to church, or to think about God. So the young preacher visited John one day and simply asked John what he owned.

John stuck out his chest and pointed in every direction. "Young man, to the east I own all of those oil wells, and to the west I own all those white-faced Hereford cattle; up north I own every stick of forest to this side of the mountains, and to the south I own every fenced pasture and lake your eyes can see."

"Now, boy! Tell me what you own."

The young preacher stood there quietly for a moment, but reassured, and answered John with a question. "John, it's better for me to explain it to you this way." Pointing upward to heaven, the young preacher asked John, 'What do you own up there?'"

John held his head down with a look of shame for a few seconds as his faced turned red, and muttered, "Guess you got me there, Preach. I don't think I've even got a small lot up there, unfortunately."

For sixteen years now my lovely, wonderful, beautiful wife and I have lived at the same residence since we moved to colorful Colorado in 1988. I remember so well a man showing me home after home day after day when I was looking for a place to live and bring my family to. I was quite pushed by our tight schedule, too, at the time, to find our little abode.

Nevertheless, day after day I looked, and I would always come back to the same house. I looked at bigger houses, and smaller houses, more expensive and less expensive, but I would always come back to that chocolate house on the corner of 618 South Laredo Circle. Why? It was just us; it was Nancy Jean, my wife. And we bought it. It is now our "old home place."

It has been a long time since I took a team of professionals and lay people from a church on a mission trip deep into the heart of Mexico. But I have gone many times. On those trips to Galeana, Mexico, just south of Monterrey, I can still envision the caves where I saw families living and making their homes. All along the Sierra Madre Mountain Range this type of dwelling still exists to this day. Their house is God-made; it's a cave. Their "old home place" which they refer to was one day scooped out by the hand of the Almighty.

We all know, or should know, that's it's really not where we live, but how we live that makes all the difference down here. Remember, the Son of God had no place to lay his head, yet there are literally thousands of homes built in his memory and for his worship here on this planet. There is one thing that I am absolutely confident of, and that is where we live reveals in the long run how we live. You may not think people take notice of you and how you live in your neighborhood, but they do. After sixteen years at the same residence we are the Johnsons who live there on the corner. It's been up to us over all these years to make our "old home place" a witness for God and His glory, and the same with you wherever you have been living. How is your "old home place" going?

ATONEMENT

"We owe nothing more."

SCARLET AND CRIMSON, SNOW AND WOOL

The Great Calculator

Just like you do, I carry a lot inside me that we wish could be eradicated with the snap of a finger. But we continue to carry that turmoil and stuff and even sin because we are unwilling to come to the table with it and really deal with it.

No one looks at this more graphically, I think, than does Isaiah of old. What a picture of wrong in people's lives! Isaiah depicts it so well as God breathes this marvelous thought into his mind and heart. He writes:

> "Come now, let us reason together," says the Lord. "Though your sins are like scarlet, they shall be as white as snow; though they are as red as crimson, they shall be as wool. If you are willing and obedient, you will eat the best from the land..." (Isaiah 1:18, 19 NIV).

Reasoning. It evolves actually from a mathematical word. It comes from the Latin word, ratio. Ratio deals with calculation, reason, rationale. How things are calculated. How they are added up in our lives.

What's the ratio of wrong going on in your mind and heart and soul? Is there some overload there? Do you find stuff that's added up over time and made the ratio out of balance? Over taxed by things that just shouldn't be in your life? And you've repressed this to the point of exhaustion.

This is the scarlet and the crimson. These represent the **stains.**

These represent the things that just won't go away. They haunt you and taunt you.

There is absolutely nothing that Satan wants to do more than get you just a little off center. A little off center on a highway, or runway, or railway, and there's a crash! I know the dark world. I know his mission statement, "to lie and to steal and to destroy and kill!"

He loves the scarlet and the crimson. He knows what it took by a loving God to be able to blot out our sins and our wrongs. But the devil is so passionate about seeing the scarlet and the crimson. Anything that will leave that stain, that red-dyed influence upon our character or disposition gives him something more to gloat over.

When the king fell, David had done so much wrong, so very much wrong. He had broken the heart of God and his own family and kingdom by committing murder and adultery. Then the prophet went to him and pointed out the scarlet and the crimson in his life:

> Nathan said to David (after David had confessed he had sinned), "The Lord also has put away your sin; you shall not die. However, because by this deed you have given great occasion to the enemies of the Lord to blaspheme...." (11 Samuel 12:13, 14 NKJV).

I guess we've all read Hawthorne's, *The Scarlet Letter*. It's such a portrayal of the stain people carry with them after they fall. Shame and disgust, even hatred and distrust, always seem to follow scarlet and crimson. It's no wonder for some, it leads to a dead end street and life is ended with guilt and despair.

But it doesn't have to be.

You and I must read Isaiah's words very carefully or we'll miss the incredible message behind these sacred lines. Why? Because **there is hope, much hope** for all of us who carry unneeded baggage.

Philip Roth has written a novel, *The Human Stain*, which is coming out in a new movie. But Hollywood also needs to capture a
forthcoming novel, *The Divine Cleaning*. When God gets through
with His ratio, His calculation, there is a way, a reasoning, a solu-
tion to all our wrongs and sins and horrible guilt.

I heard a very famous international preacher recently who was tour-
ing our nation. He said the two greatest events in all of human
history are: one, the birth of Christ (God incarnate, coming to this
earth in human flesh), and two, the fact that Christ came out of His
tomb in a new, resurrected body.

I'm sorry, but I beg to differ with this great communicator. Although these two events were a must in the redemption of mankind
from his sins, to me he missed the most important event in history.
And this was the payment, that priceless gift and inexplicable sacrifice of His Son's blood on the cross of Calvary.

No one, and I mean no one, can ever even begin to imagine or even
attempt to explain such an event in human history. We know what
materialistic stuff costs: what a house or car or boat or suit or watch
costs. But how do you price God's Son's own blood? Not to men-
tion the enormous, unthinkable love God gave at that moment;
how do you value such?

Would you give up your child or grandchild for just one other
person's sins and guilt? Be honest, would you? Probably not, nor
would I. But somehow not only did God give up His only son for
all of us, but when Christ's blood was offered upon that old tree, a
payment was made which provided a free and clear indebtedness
for you and me. We owe nothing more. We are made whole in
Him. No debt! No scarlet! No crimson!

Most people cannot accept such a free gift, such freedom itself. It
is too good to be true. "I must have to do something to attain this
grace."

In a small letter to early Christians St. John wrote:

Here, then, is the message which we heard from him, and now proclaim to you: God is Light and no shadow of darkness can exist in him. Consequently, if we were to say that we enjoyed fellowship with him and still went on living in darkness, we should be both telling and living a lie. But if we are really living in the same light in which he eternally exists, then we have true fellowship with each other, and the blood which son Jesus shed for us **keeps us clean from all sin**. If we refuse to admit that we are sinners, then we live in a world of illusion and the truth becomes a stranger to us. But if we really admit that we have sinned, we find him reliable and just—-**he forgives our sins and makes us thoroughly clean** from all that is evil. For if we say "we have not sinned, we are making him a liar and cut ourselves off from what he has to say to us." (1 John 1:5-10 (J. B. Phillips Translation).

It's been years now since I walked out of my office and just went to a park in Denver and started walking upon the fresh, new, fallen snow from the night before. Not a single person had entered the park where I went; I stood there all alone. It was an early morn hour, too. And the snow looked like white, pristine cake icing across the floor of this little park. My footprints were totally distinct. Every step I took I could look back and see those imprints in the white snow. You know, a new snow is so very, very perfectly white, too.

In fact, when the sun gets up that beautiful white snow becomes blinding to our eyes as it reflects those rays toward us. That's just how white and pure and clean it can be.

Even as I drove away that day from that park I could see from quite a distance, those footprints I had made in that white snow. That whiteness, that icing, that covering is what God is all about, really. "Come let us reason together," scarlet, crimson, stains, mistakes, hurts, heartaches, foolish blunders, stupid choices we've made, and God says I'll make you "whiter than snow and pure as wool."

I can't speak for you, but I have been so privileged to have felt His refreshing, **awesome grace**. I am no different from you; we have just sinned differently, all of us—"for all have sinned and come short of God's glory." But I do know, when He gets hold of us and blots out all that scarlet and crimson there are no more stains, no more sins in His sight. We are free, clean, **totally clean**, too. The Great Calculator knows what you and I need, and He can change the very worst of us. What wonder! What fantastic wonder! No stain and no shame! No more crimson by His great redemption! So come **let us reason together**, there's **hope** for you and for me.

"... don't you just feel better and cleaner when you get with God in prayer"

WHITER THAN SNOW

It was Christmas time. We had just moved to Denver. My wife's family joined us for the holiday. It was very cold, and a big snow had come just before Christmas. I think it was 1989.

Both her parents were alive then. It was like a reunion. The children, our son and daughter, were much younger then.

I remember just like it was yesterday, too. Nancy's sister's family had come. Their three girls and the whole bunch of us went sledding at a nearby hill.

Boy, was it cold. Frigid! Snow was everywhere, and it was thick. We must have gotten eight inches or so that week.

Laura, our daughter, had an old sled that I had bought the summer before at a garage sale. It wasn't one of these new modern plastic sleds. It was made of real wood with steel sled blades, and had steel bar sides. We still have it in the basement of our home.

Somehow as I pushed the forth or fifth time on the little sled for one of the kids to race down the hill, a loose screw caught my hand and cut a gash instantly out of my skin. I felt the sudden pain, but didn't say anything to anyone because I didn't want to upset the children. Blood just gushed forth out of my hand—I couldn't even get my handkerchief out soon enough. So I told Terry, (Nancy's sister's husband) that I had to run back home, and I'd be back "in a sec or two."

As I ran back toward the house I felt very faint; in fact, I stopped for a moment or two and put my head between my legs so I wouldn't pass out. A lot of things race through your mind when things like this happen, when in reality it's usually never a serious thing at all.

You just think it is, or it might be.

After I ran about a hundred yards or so it was like a voice spoke to me and said, "Just stop and take your handkerchief off your hand and stick your hand into the ice cold snow—then the bleeding will stop."

When this voice came to me, I looked to my left and there was a row of bushes that were covered with thick snow on top of them. And I just rammed my hand into the ice cold snow and just held it there as long as I could take it. Man, was it cold.

When I finally could not stand it any longer I pulled my almost frozen hand from the snow, and now I know why the voice spoke to me. It was a message that was twofold. One, it was a message from the Lord to my mind simply to use common sense—cold contracts. And the bleeding stopped. Secondly, this voice from the Lord was very obvious to me when it was all over. I realized for the first time in my life just what Christ's atoning blood is all about. Whether a person is a Christian or not they have to wonder about this historical figure who gave his life for the sins of the world almost 2,000 years ago.

I looked into the snow that bright sunshiny day and it dawned upon me just how white, white really is. The crimson flow of blood was such a dramatic contrast to the white snow that it was startling, literally startling to my heart. I've never seen that much white, never before, nor since.

Then I remembered so well that man, David, who had done it all wrong. He used his kingship to take advantage of a commander in his own army and even commit adultery with the man's wife. And on top of that he murdered him, or had him murdered in battle.

It was after that he had sinned so blatantly and foolishly and stupidly that Nathan, the prophet, went to David and confronted him with his evil and inexcusable behavior. Nathan asked David what should be done to a rich man who took advantage of a poor man.

He said the rich man took the poor man's prized lamb so he could feed one of his special friends who was traveling through.

In David's anger he exclaimed that this man should die. I'm sure that if you know any Bible history, you know that David's life and kingdom were never the same afterwards. But more than this, this man after God's own heart, admitted that he had sinned against God.

I think it was probably soon after this interview with Nathan that David hid himself and took his pen and began to write those moving and stirring words in his 51st Psalm:

Have mercy upon me, O God, according to your loving kindness: according unto the multitude of your tender mercies blot out my transgressions...Against You and You only have I sinned, and done this evil in your sight...Purge me with hyssop, and I shall be clean: wash me, and I shall be whiter than snow. "

Now I know, now I understand, what is whiter than snow. But it took that incident where I placed my bleeding hand into the snow to understand just how clean God is and how clean God can make us in His sight. And it's all done through that man who really did give His life blood upon that tree on the hill called Calvary.

My late father-in-law was truly the most godly man I've ever known upon this earth. He is the only man I've ever known that even ungodly men felt uncomfortable telling a nasty joke in his presence. He walked so close to God that you just couldn't get around him without feeling the presence of the living God in his simple, but very spiritual life.

One day Lloyd commented to me on something I will take to my grave. You know, one of those things that you store in the computer of your brain forever. He said, "Ronnie, don't you just feel better and cleaner when you get with God in prayer? You know, there's just nothing like getting with Him (the Lord) and just confessing all of your sins and wrongs to him. When you really get alone with Him and share your heart with Him you just feel all clean and good inside; in fact, your day and week seems to even go better."

Yes it does...yes it does.

Do you remember singing that old hymn, *Grace Greater Than Our Sin*? With all the newer songs we sing today in church I miss singing this one a lot. Julia H. Johnston wrote this and it was copyrighted in 1910. One of those marvelous verses says it all, I think:

> Dark is the stain that we cannot hide,
> What can avail to wash it away?
> Look! There is flowing a crimson tide—
> Whiter than snow you may be today.
>
> Grace, grace, God's grace,
> Grace that will pardon and cleanse within;
> Grace, grace, God's grace,
> Grace that is greater than all our sin!

Boy! What grace and what forgiveness! And what a wonderful spiritual principle we can claim. As black as our sins are, as black as our wrongs can be, as black as our mistakes, through Christ and His shed blood on the cross we can be made whiter than snow. Believe me, I've seen just how white that white is, too.

What comfort and assurance! No matter who you are and what you've done, there is hope for your greatest failures in life and your greatest sins. And yes, you can be made whiter than snow.

PRAISE

"(The Lord) is present tense."

THE LORD IS.....

The Lord means not just any Lord. There needs to be a **The** in front of this Person. He is The One, The Way, The Truth and The Life. This **The** before Lord is right. He is not just another god on this earth. But He is **The** Lord.

The Lord, El. In Hebrew it is in the very first line of the Bible. In the beginning El (Elheem: God). It is that root term for God, Lord. The El is my Shepherd. The One who is Ruler of all things. He is Lord of lords and King of kings. The Lord, the Master, the Sovereign is my shepherd. He controls all; He owns all. Remember, if He is hungry He doesn't have to ask us because "He owns the cattle upon thousand hills"(Psalm 50:10).

The Lord is present tense. He is right this moment my Shepherd. What an august thought! The Lord is this very moment my Shepherd. I don't have to wait in line, be placed on hold, or go through a menu to get to Him. He is my Shepherd every split second of the day. Wow!   He is not gonna be, perhaps so, or maybe he will— No! He is my Shepherd. I can turn to Him this very moment in my need or distress.

The Lord is my, that's right, my own **Shepherd**. The same God who created me and breathed life into my nostrils is my own personal God, Savior, Friend, and Shepherd. Although invisible, He is my daily companion and friend and confidant. He is not made from some human mold and sitting inside a handmade statue or ornate tomb. But He is alive and inside me and is my own Lord and Shepherd to help me everyday when I turn to Him. He is my Shepherd, my own personal, intimate Comforter for such a chaotic world in which I live.

I shall not want. He really does fulfill my heart and soul. He is a Father to me when I feel lonely, a Friend to me when I am in need. He is a Supporter to me when I go through sickness and sorrow. I *want* only when I get away from Him and His presence; only then do I feel a real drought in my soul. But He fulfills; He makes me feel complete, strong, and confident. He rescues me with His mighty arms, and in Him I *want* no more. He satisfies my inner self. I feel His presence and great assurance. You don't *want* when you're fed, when you're full.

He makes me to lie down in green pastures. He secures my resting places. He knows when I need the refreshment of rest and revitalization. My Shepherd has a way of stopping me in my tracks at times and putting me on my back. But in the end I am renewed through proper rest and sleep. In Him I can sleep well. He makes me feel good. Rested. Rejuvenated.

He leads me beside the still waters. He knows when I need quietness. He knows how to rekindle my spirit in solitude. So He leads me beside those places that are quiet, still waters, soothing experiences that heal my noisy life. He directs my life toward recuperation in a restless world in which I live. And I bathe in the quiet. I sense His presence and His healing. He knows what is best for me. Nothing is loud. Just quiet, still waters.

He restores my soul. My soul is me. He works on me. He cares about me, about you, about our own little world. He sands away the rust. He puts a fresh, new coat of paint on my life. He takes time for me—an assembly line work—He does us by hand. He nails in those loose nails, re-roofs my heart and soul. He restores me to my original strength and stamina. He reconditions my whole self. I am uplifted by His enormous power. He gives me new wind under my wings. I am able now to soar after being down and discouraged. What a Restorer He is!

He leads me in the paths of righteousness for his name's sake. There is no other name like Jehovah's name. He not only knows the right path for me, but He is **the path** of life. As I stay on His path I find that His life is life more abundantly in which to live. As He leads I follow and I discover more and more about His shepherding abilities. He is my Mapquest on these dark, wet, slippery streets called life. He knows how to navigate my life around those deadly icebergs on the stormy seas, too. He leads me not only around danger, but points me toward paths that give me a **high** like no other. But then, why not? He is El, Lord, King and Almighty!

Yea, though I walk through the valley of the shadow of death I will fear no evil, for thou art with me. The assumption is made - I will face sorrow. Valleys can get real dark for us; they are often totally hidden from the sun. They can be colder, lonelier, darker and more dangerous than any other terrain. Valleys just have the smell of death and foreboding danger. But my Captain, my El (Lord) is beside me and in me and leading me. So my fears and anxieties are abolished. I feel safe in Him, and I am safe in Him. He carries me at times. He knows my fears. He knows my Achilles heel. I am not exhausted because of His faithful presence; I feel the nudge of His staff— I just know He's around as I move through those treacherous valleys of death and looming doom.

Thy rod and Thy staff, they comfort me. You provide the tools for my well-being and security. You, my Shepherd, are always reaching out to me and I feel your arm of deliverance. I can look back on my years on this green earth and remember how you salvaged me and all my hopes and dreams; how You brought me safely over those crisis times of sheer desperation. You've been the One to help me "stick it out" when I was the one who wanted to "give in." Your rod and staff have been my armor, shield and strength against the enemy who is ever present to oppress and destroy.

You prepare a table before me in the presence of my enemies. Boy! Do I have them, too. Don't you? They are always present. But You're always **providing** for me and for others. You're just always there. Always! Even in the face of my worst encounters on this globe, You are making those incredible provisions for my betterment. How you love me! Why? That itself is a huge mystery. But You do, I know. In the highest threats that come and slam against my life, You show up, always, always! What's funny is, I know You will show up, too. You just never leave me nor forsake me, just like you promised. Wow! Thanks for those meals even in the presence of those who would love to bring me down, or see me fall on my face.

You anoint my head with oil… My what soothing, soothing blessings you bestow upon me. Your blessings make me fat. The good kind of fat, too, with wave after wave of inspirations and wonders from Your mighty hand. They are truly countless, just like the sand that is upon the seashore. Your ever-present Spirit gives me such reassurance through friends and little notes, through unexpected phone calls of concern and mercy-drop blessings day after day. No wonder the Psalmist declared, "You daily load us with blessings" (Psalm 68:19). My head, my thoughts cannot help but praise You for all that You do. I pray, "Lord, keep the oil flowing upon me, keep your healing and anointing coming my way; You know how inadequate I am without You."

My cup runneth over. Why? Because you care about me when no one else will. You love me in spite of my stupid, sinful mistakes.   You come to my aid when all others forsake me. You understand the person you've made like no other. My cup really can't hold any more; You have overwhelmed me with family and friends and fun and prosperity. You have brought me (man) together with You (God); by grace through faith that has zoomed into **a life relationship** like no other. No wonder my cup can't contain Your spiritual fortunes which You send my way. They are inexhaustible. I am rich in every way because of You, Father, and what You've poured into my little cup. Thanks. Thanks so much. I am full because of you.

Surely goodness and mercy shall follow me all the days of my life: Wow! Again.! What a prayer! I think I want the same prayer. I do. Surely goodness, the bountiful, pleasant things of life will come my way. And mercy––God only knows we all need this. I need Your divine favor, Your great, kind, pity upon me. For we have "all like sheep gone astray." May my Shepherd Lord impart goodness and mercy upon my life and yours. When I breathe my last breath and my work is over down here, may I be able to look back and see His goodness and His mercy that He showed to me all the days and years of my life. My, my, my, what a prayer!

And I will dwell in the house of the Lord forever. I sense absolutely no hesitation or remorse or lack of confidence here. "I know Whom I have believed, and am persuaded that He is able to keep that which I have committed unto Him against that day" (2 Timothy 1:12 KJV). I have a winter home and a summer home there; a mansion to live in, **forever**. One day I shall see His face and so shall you. Only then will I really know the Shepherd that truly is and has been. The Lord is my Shepherd I shall not.

However high the mountain is that you are facing in your life today, the Supreme Shepherd can guide you over. He knows every single little problem you are facing. Turn to the Shepherd and you'll hear that voice remind you "The Lord is my Shepherd I shall not want."

"He is the key to victory."

BRAZEN

For whatever reason, sometimes we move in a direction only God can understand. Don't you sometimes just go off in a direction that even you question yourself, "Why am I doing this?" But you and I do it anyway. And then we wonder over it.

I was teaching recently on a cruise ship along with my associate. After one of our evening sessions I went to dinner and then something led me right to the front of the cruise ship. The evening was perfect, I mean just perfect, too.

I just felt like going to the top of the ship and looking out over the inlet that we were passing through in Alaska. I actually stood there all alone; surprisingly, there was not a soul in sight. That's right, out of over 3,000 people onboard the *Norwegian Sky*, I found the whole front of this ship to myself. I feel like God gave me this half hour or so just to be with Him and His mighty creation.

I actually spread my arms out like the young man in the Titanic movie and just took in the evening breeze and that august presence of the Almighty and His incredible creation before me. To my left a whale flapped his tail daringly into the air and in front of me one sprayed water high into the air. It dawned upon me that we were treading into their native territory. My God, what a scene!

Surrounded by those spiraling fir trees that paraded ever so close upon the mountains in sight, I could only smell the purest air I have ever breathed upon this planet. In the far background stood those pristine snow-capped jaded mountains that seem to be looking over the shoulder of the others. It must have been around 9 P.M. in the evening, past my bedtime when I am at home in Denver.

Honestly, I talked to El (The Lord), and other times I stood there absolutely speechless. Then suddenly to my right came two gorgeous bald eagles flying side by side, along the right side of this giant cruise ship. As I watched them I noticed that they were joining a flock. That's right, a whole flock of other bald eagles that were swooping down into the water to catch the thousands of fish that were swirling in the water before me.

Getting the picture? Wow! The water itself had a mystic look about it this June evening in the Last Frontier. The waters were dark and yet a glittering of that ever present sunlight that seems to hover over the horizon. This brought on an unspeakable silhouetted evening I shall never forget. No man could ever look upon this and doubt His faithful and divine handiwork. They are kidding themselves. Come on!

He is the Master of artists, the most able of all architects, the most able of all engineers. No man ever will design such in his laboratory. For whatever reason, God gave me this time with Him and His enormous presence. No wonder He told Moses of old when Moses questioned Him about what he should say when they asked who sent him. Remember? Do you remember? God said just tell them I AM that I AM has sent you. He just is. He can't explain it any better than that. He is just Who He is, and that's just the opposite of all of us—we want to be something so bad. But we're not. We want to be, but He is who He is and none other.

If You Only Knew Him

Oh how I wish I could just tell you,
How much He means to me;
But I feel sometimes I'm not the one to tell,
Because I am nothing like Him nor ever will be.

Oh how I wish that you could know,
Just for one moment in time;
If you could only experience His grace,
You would never want to change your mind.

Yes, now it's just a memory, but I shall carry this scene to my grave. It was one of those reminders that if God can make all of this in the wild, if He can so orchestrate such magnificent scenes of nature and creativity, this God, this El (Lord), can do any darn thing He wants to any time He gets ready to. Never underestimate your little, weak, doubting, frail prayers. This Jehovah God is big, real big. He can do anything you want Him to if He decides to give the go ahead. And I mean anything! He is as brazen as He chooses. Never thought of God as brazen until I experienced this.

Yeah! We're different from Him. When He walked this old earth He knew every step He was taking. But sometime we don't really know where we're going or even where we've been. But Jesus knew every step He was taking to the cross. This is why we need a Savior. This is why we need Him and each other. Because He also knew every step He was taking out of that grave as well. He is the key to victory.

Going somewhere? Just where are you going? Are you just moving in a direction that only God knows where you're going? I do hope you get to see what this author has seen. No words can really describe it. Thank you, Father, for Your surprises—you're a great Dad.

ANGELS

"... those angels are there."

SHROUD OF THE UNSEEN

Only now and then do any of us experience this, but it does happen. You can deny it if you will, but this is more real than the air you breathe and the sun that rises from the east each morning. For years I have experienced the reality of the Shroud of the Unseen. No, it's not an everyday excursion or incident. But I am as convinced of this as anything that I believe in.

Angelic presence does not have to be in some heavenly or super-natural form or body to accomplish his or her purpose. Often we want to refer to angelic beings as a he or an it...I'm convinced that angelic presence could be in a "her" as well. The word angel or angels are used 294 times in scripture. Both in Hebrew and Greek the word means, messenger.

The very nature of angels is most interesting. Just to name a few, they are: intelligent and wise (2 Samuel 14:20; 19:27); heavenly spirit beings (Psalm 104:4); higher than men (Psalm 8:5); need no rest (Revelation 4:8); can eat food (Genesis 18:8); and they can speak languages (I Corinthians 13:1).

St. Paul reminded us that angels can take on the form of a real tangible body. Remember he declared, "Be not forgetful to enter-tain strangers: for thereby some have entertained angels unawares" (Hebrews 13:2).

The Shroud of the Unseen (angelic presence) is that mysterious person we meet in life whom we have never encountered before and in our crisis they are just there. Either they are helping place our body on a stretcher, holding our hand in an auto accident, plac-ing that one person in our path who just knows what to do for us like no other soul in this whole-wide world, or that little word of comfort that comes to us through a note, a verse of scripture or some thought that just jumps out and grabs our heart and inspires us with a confidence that could come from no other.

Yes, I believe in angel presence and power. The same God that threw this universe together, and only He knows how many more, can afford us, His own creatures, to encourage us and aid us and ensure that we are not alone down here in this big world of billions of people. The Bible says that they were created by Christ before the Earth (Job 38:4-7; Psalm 148:2-5; Colossians 1:16).

Tomorrow when you get up and go to work as usual, or if you're retired, you will go about your usual schedule. This shroud of the unseen is just not something you and I will look around every corner hoping to see. But behind the shroud are living, active real creatures who represent both good and bad. Having been a pastor for many years I have dealt with those angelic beings and their dark presence on many occasions. I could write volumes on the evil, demonic experiences that I have encountered over many decades.

Probably one of the paramount experiences I had was with a young man and woman who lived across the street from both the home and the church where I once lived and pastored. Once he chased her with a hatchet trying to cut her head off. They lived in little more than a shack. They were very poor and did the drug scene.

One night my wife, Nancy, was out of town. I was asleep and she had taken the children with her on a trip. In the middle of the night I was awakened by screams which I shall never forget; the young woman was cursing to the top of her lungs. I have never heard such language before nor since, nor have I ever seen such sheer anger and hatred in the face of a human being. The noise was so loud that it sounded like she was on a megaphone a cheerleader would use at an outdoor ballgame.

She wouldn't stop. She, in fact, couldn't stop. Such a demonic force overtook her, I could tell she was so possessed that it was a Satanic spirit within her. You just don't forget things like this. An experience is never at the mercy of an argument. And I experienced this that awful summer evening.

When I finally went to the window to try to discern what she was saying and at whom she was swearing, I saw her red, glaring face looking right at me, and yes it was me who she was lambasting. Honestly, the veins in her neck were visibly strained at fifty yards away. I had never even met her before. She and her young husband had just moved into the small community some months earlier.

I shall never forget, I stayed awake most of that night and tried to pray for her release from such demonic power in her life. It was an awful experience for me, but one that made me well aware of those people who are evil in every way. No wonder that Greek word for devil, diabolos, means adversary, accuser and slanderer.

On the contrary, over the years I have met people whom I have been enormously blessed by their angelic influence. You just know that they were God-sent. The timing of their coming into my life, their incredible influence, their aid and support were beyond the ordinary. They have been messengers, what I call the shroud of the unseen—no doubt whatsoever.

When I first started out in pastoral ministry I went to a church at the young age of twenty years old. The church had just split over a power struggle between two very strong-willed leaders and the group that followed them. I later learned that at one point half of the congregation was meeting in one end of the church and the other half was meeting in the other end. I will make it short—it was a hell of a mess to say the least! To add to this dilemma, the prior minister could not make up his mind if he had been saved (converted to Christ) or not. So he had been baptized over a course of about three years at least four or five times. Imagine going to a church like this at the age of twenty as the senior pastor.

Honestly, I almost had a breakdown. There are no words to describe how miserable I became. About this time a man came along in my life and I can only vaguely remember him now after all the years. But he would call me up and take me for a lengthy ride and buy me lunch and just talk to me and encourage my life. God forgive me, I do not even remember his name. But I do remember his love and aid and support and those refreshing trips he would take me on and just buy me lunch. What an angel!

I would pour out my heart to him, and he would listen and express the most awesome concern a person would ever want. Always when I returned I was energized, encouraged and ready to fight the battle again. He was a very special messenger to me.

In scripture angels appeared to: Abraham, Moses, Jacob, Joshua, David, Elijah, Elisha, Daniel, Joseph, Mary, to Peter, John, Phillip, and Paul and to others. The shroud of the unseen, the veil is there, the mystery; those angels are there. Today, tomorrow and until time ends, they keep you and me on their list; we are forever running into their loving, caring, empathetic arms.

"Nanna," our five-year-old grandson asked recently as we were scurrying down the highway, "Who made dirt?"

Nanna replied, "God did, Davin. God has a lot of mysteries which we don't understand, but He's made everything, me and you and PaPa."

Yeah! Davin, that's right, I thought to myself, He's made a lot things which we just don't understand. You know, like Seraphims and Cherubims and heavenly creatures that you won't buy at a Wal-Mart store. But you never know, you might meet one. Yep! He made dirt, and he made angels, too.

A Final Thought From the Author...

Today you and I live in a world fractured by discriminations, terrorists, corporate scandals, a volatile economy, nuclear threats and unending crime. We also live in a world midst so much unrest and shakiness where love has never been needed more. You are loved, too. You may feel at times you are different from other people, kind of "singled out". But you have the same challenges, deal with the same world issues that your neighbor does next door.

You really are loved, too. Be reaffirmed in the great truth—God loves you more than words can say.

Perhaps the greatest lie in this life is the lie that the devil wants you to believe; that you are inferior, worthless and a composite of self-doubt. No one wants you to love yourself less than Satan does. His greatest success comes when he can "make dirt out of your life". The people who live paralyzed by fear and stupid mistakes which have marred their character, their truth and their lives forever do so as a result of Satan's awesome persuasions.

I have written this book to bring assurance to you. Comfort. Healing. Hope. Yes, you, especially you. You are loved too. God has spent more to express this unbelievable love and incomparable grace than any other riches or assets known to mankind. I hope you have felt this love by reading these chapters. Why? Because…

YOU ARE LOVED, TOO.